False Prophets Can Kill You

False Accusations of Sex and Murder

"Beware of false prophets, which come to you in sheep's
clothing, but inwardly they are ravening wolves."...Jesus
(Matthew 7:15 KJV)

Tony C. Little

WESTBOW®
P R E S S
A DIVISION OF THOMAS NELSON
& ZONDERVAN

Cover designed by Superior Graphics Company and The Taylorsville Times
Scripture taken from the King James Version of the Bible

WestBow Press books may be ordered through booksellers or by contacting:

WestBow Press
A Division of Thomas Nelson & Zondervan
1663 Liberty Drive
Bloomington, IN 47403
www.westbowpress.com
1 (866) 928-1240

ISBN: 978-1-4908-5654-4 (sc)
ISBN: 978-1-4908-5655-1 (hc)
ISBN: 978-1-4908-5656-8 (e)

Library of Congress Control Number: 2014918400

Printed in the United States of America

WestBow Press rev. date: 11/18/2014

CONTENTS

ACKNOWLEDGMENTS

It would be almost impossible to acknowledge all the people who helped me on this project. There were many preachers, deacons, Sunday School teachers, friends and family that contributed to this work. This happened over a period of more than seven years.

I have to mention the person who was without doubt the very best contributor. Her untiring dedication and caring work was unsurpassable. She is my wonderful wife and my best friend, Priscilla. I haven't known anyone with as much love, compassion and understanding.

Every good and perfect gift comes from God. Anyone can achieve all things through Christ, who strengthens us. Jesus told his disciples: you can do nothing without me. God helped me with this story and made it possible. He helps us do everything. I must acknowledge God first and foremost. He inspires to heights we never imagined. We must love and obey Him and love people. This is following Jesus, and it's the essence of salvation! If any good comes from this story, our God in heaven will have all the credit. He is the only reason we exist. If we acknowledge Him, He will direct our paths forever.

DEDICATION

Karen's life inspired people. She tried her best to live a good life. She loved everyone. Her intense desire for more of God, led to the events described in this story.

Karen was a wonderful wife, mother, and grandmother. She was also the answer to my prayers. A few weeks before Karen died, she made it crystal clear how much she loved me. It was as if she was preparing me for the tragedy of her loss. A part of her will remain with me forever.

This book is for Karen Hendren Little. I believe she has many rewards in heaven for how she inspired people to a higher level. Karen did her part to promote the kingdom of God. I'm thankful for the twenty years we had together.

PREFACE

This story can help people learn from mistakes Karen and I made in religion and marriage. People should realize when something is wrong in their religion. Mistakes are acceptable; we all make them. Of course our mistakes should be small and not terrible. Religion should be a calm and peaceful experience; often it isn't. The history of religion isn't pleasant. Millions of people have suffered and died. Religion has caused many wars and confusion. It could lead to stress that becomes overwhelming. Karen was stressed over her religion and false prophets. Religion can be good or a horrifying experience.

Religious people killed Jesus Christ. Jesus loved them enough to reveal their mistakes and expose their evil. Jesus let them know the devil was their father, not God. He explained their teachings were wrong, like many generations before them. He proclaimed their traditions went against His Word and led people into hell. Jesus didn't give special treatment to religious people; He rebuked the scribes and Pharisees on many occasions.

Any religion that teaches kindness, love, forgiveness, and peace toward mankind, teaches what Jesus instructed. Most people in every religion, actually believe these are things they accomplish. People should be honest with themselves. They need to ask these questions. Are we doing these things or not? Do we follow Jesus Christ, or false doctrines and wrong traditions?

I desired to tell this story and possibly save people's lives. Many false teachings are exposed in our religion and others. People must not follow others blindly, but study God's Word for themselves. False prophets lead people astray with wrong traditions. People should realize religion could send them to hell. Evil spirits use anything to destroy people. God holds us accountable if we allow this. We can understand the Bible, if we ask God for help.

The sudden death of Karen prompted me to write this. The Holy Spirit touched me in a special way and helped with this most difficult journey. God inspired me to study His Word extensively. Not being a college educated person, I had to educate myself. After printing almost all this by hand, I purchased a computer. In essence, I went back to school. The lessons we learn the hard way, make the more lasting impressions.

Without a doubt the Bible was my best source of reference. A concordance and dictionary were most helpful. A good PC Bible study program proved invaluable. I highly recommend these things to anyone, especially to teachers and preachers. Prayer, meditation, and council from other Christians were absolutely necessary.

We need inspiration to write, or do anything of significance. Nothing inspires like the tragic loss of someone you love—except of course the Holy Spirit. He is always my main source of inspiration.

The reason I wrote this story is—I was involved. Religion paralyzes and brainwashes, when misconstrued by false prophets. It causes confusion and many problems. "And be not conformed to this world: but be ye transformed by the renewing of your mind, that ye may prove what is that good, and acceptable, and perfect will of God." (Rom. 12:2) Nothing will renew a person's mind like studying God's Word!

Please learn from my experiences in life. It's great when we learn from mistakes of others and avoid suffering. I hope people study God's Word, follow Jesus and understand spiritual matters. This helps us have success, peace, love and happiness. Discover the abundant life Jesus spoke of in John 10:10.

No one understands everything about spiritual matters. God wants it that way, so we'll live by faith. He reveals what we need to know, when it's necessary. Everyone should remember, we have to work out our own salvation with fear and trembling. I'm paraphrasing Philippians 2:12. It's easy to interpret or rightly divide some scriptures. Many don't believe that verse—or many others. Some believe almost anything. We are overly optimistic at times and believe the too good to be true teachings. Wrong traditions sound wonderful—on the surface. If they don't line up with the Bible, avoid them like a plague.

Scriptures taken out of context create false teachings. An attempt to make God's Word line up with false doctrines is a serious mistake. It causes the misinterpretation of scriptures that children can understand. This religious practice causes people to take away from the words found in God's Word. Some misinterpret large portions of the Bible. Many do this, but that doesn't make it right. There is one who is always right—God. He is three persons with many Spirits. He knows us more than we know ourselves!

Don't follow anyone blindly and rely on someone else to determine where you will spend eternity. These are essential matters of life and death. There are false teachings in most religions and none is perfect. Any endeavor sought by people is flawed because we aren't perfect. God made mankind perfect, but allowed us to fall to realize the need for His help. God's Spirit guides us, if we listen. Hopefully, we'll learn how to hear His voice and not listen to evil spirits as they try to destroy us.

If you gain nothing else from this story, I hope and pray you will study God's Word and apply the awesome truths. If you do, God will approve of you. You can have Christ in you, the hope of glory. Jesus Christ is King of kings and Lord of all lords. I believe He is returning soon; don't be left behind.

CHAPTER ONE

WHEN DID ALL THIS BEGIN

I met Karen in 1986. Her life changing experience happened before we met. One night in church, she desired the baptism of the Holy Ghost. Someone prayed for Karen, laid hands on her, and she fell to the floor. She spoke a language which couldn't be understood, other tongues.

Two hours later, her pastor drove Karen's car to her home, while Karen and his wife followed in their car. Karen was drunk in the Spirit. She was staggering and laughing. Unaware of how late it was, she woke her neighbor, the pastor of her childhood church. The preacher was excited and wished his church would receive the baptism. He asked Karen to explain her experience at their next service. After the service, a meeting was held in a classroom. Some received the same experience, although not as dramatic as Karen.

I've wondered over the last twenty years why some are intensely affected by this baptism and others aren't. Perhaps it's proportionate to past hurts, or how much one hungers after God's righteousness. It's possibly a combination of both or emotionalism. The baptism is genuine and shouldn't be misused.

Karen was married for ten years. They had a daughter and son. Karen and her former husband were married before they graduated high school. They endured long intervals of separation. These troublesome times were difficult for Karen and her daughter. The girl was hospitalized because of severe stomach pains. Thank God, it was nothing serious, just stress from the turmoil.

When a family lacks love and affection, something must fill the emptiness. Sometimes love is misdirected toward someone else in an improper manner. Other times, God fills this void. Karen turned to God during her first marriage. Some think it's appropriate to become obsessed with God. This obsession causes some to neglect people. If we don't love people properly, we don't love God. You'll discover this as you study all five chapters in 1 John and Matthew chapter five. We might love everyone, but fail to develop a proper love toward certain people. Karen struggled with this. I had the same problem.

When Karen's husband and another woman moved in together, it was the death of their marriage. Not surprisingly, a man began to date Karen. He fell passionately in love with her. The man bought Karen anything, to win her affection. She didn't love him, but the attention was welcome. Something happened to upset their friendship. (me)

I made similar mistakes in my first marriage. The same religious spirit that got into Karen, got in me. It's amazing how some are obsessed with God and neglect people. I'm certain this isn't right. We must love others or we don't love God properly. This can be verified, in the Gospel of John and especially in 1st, and 2nd, John.

In 1985, my life dramatically changed. After ten years of marriage with my first wife, lots of parties and alcohol, I needed a huge change. I received the baptism into Jesus Christ. It's called born-again or saved.

There are different baptisms found in the Bible. However, the Bible also teaches there is one baptism in Ephesians 4:5. All the biblical baptisms are contained in the main baptism, into Jesus Christ. "...Know ye not, that so many of us as were baptized into Jesus Christ were baptized into his death?" (Rom. 6:3) We shouldn't deny the baptism of repentance, Moses, John, Jesus, into His death, of water, by fire, Holy Spirit, or the Holy Ghost. These biblical baptisms are great and should be ongoing.

We shouldn't deny any Spirit of God: Spirit of glory, Spirit of truth, Spirit of wisdom, Holy Spirit, Holy Ghost, the Father and His Son. These

2

are probably the seven Spirits of God in Revelation 3:1. The Comforter is the Spirit of truth. Take a look at Ephesians 4:4–6. "There is one body, and one Spirit, even as ye are called in one hope of your calling; One Lord, one faith, one baptism, One God and Father of all, who is above all, and through all, and in you all." Like the baptisms, all the Spirits of God are contained within the main one, (the Father). The Spirits of God are like the same or comparable, with each one having different functions. Our Heavenly Father is surely multifaceted!

Most people are confused about God having different Spirits and the three entities of God: Father, Son, Spirit. Water can be different forms and still be water. It's a liquid, but can become a solid or gas. It's frozen into ice, boiled into steam, forms clouds, but it's still water. God is much more than three. The Spirits of God are never-ending and so is He. The most amazing thing about God is—He sent His only Son to suffer and die to become the perfect sacrifice for us.

Jesus Can Save You

Getting saved is confessing and admitting to God, we have sinned. We sincerely ask Him to forgive and save us. We must be willing to follow Him. (obey) We must believe He saves—when we ask. This last part is called our faith. It's written in His Word, "But without faith it is impossible to please Him..." This is located in the first part of Hebrews 11:6. Faith in Jesus is why we're called believers. Jesus is the only way to the Father. (God) "There is a way which seemeth right unto a man; but the end thereof are the ways of death." (Prov. 14:12) Don't choose any of the wrong ways; only one way works.

Receiving Jesus Christ for salvation or our born-again experience is necessary for going to heaven. Immediately we receive the baptism of the Holy Spirit. Repentance causes this. It may not be necessary to have the baptism of the Holy Ghost with the evidence of speaking in tongues, to make it to heaven. It doesn't imply this in the Bible. Tongues is the least gift and love is a more excellent way. God gives gifts as He wills. "But all these worketh that one and the selfsame Spirit, dividing to every man severally as he will." (1 Cor. 12:11)

The baptism of the Holy Ghost provides help in many ways. To many, it becomes a private type of closet prayer. He, the Holy Spirit or Holy Ghost, gives people comfort, peace, power, joy, and love. He builds up our most Holy faith. (Jude 1:20 paraphrased)

1 Corinthians 12, 13 and 14 could enlighten you on this subject. The chapters must be interpreted right, to gain valuable insight from God. Don't let old traditions negate the Word of God. Remember, because your family believes something, that doesn't make it true. It's dangerous to deny any biblical baptism, or anything in His Word. We lean on our understanding at times. Remember the scripture Proverbs 3:5–6. "Trust in the Lord with all thine heart; and lean not unto thine own understanding. In all thy ways acknowledge him, and he shall direct thy paths." This is one of my favorites. Jesus said, "I am the way..." (1st part of John 14:6)

If a preacher believes the same as your parents, grandparents and most of your church, it doesn't make it true. Ask God to help you find the truth. "...And ye shall know the truth and the truth shall make you free." (John 8:32) Jesus said that. When we find Jesus, we find the truth.

After my conversion, my first wife must have sensed a loss of my love. I became excited about my faith, shared it frequently and with too much enthusiasm. I annoyed my wife and others. If anything isn't done with love it's in vain. 1 Corinthians 13 is the love chapter; it explains love. Love is the most important thing of all. God is love! If religious zeal isn't shown with love, it's no different than the scribes and Pharisees. Jesus viewed them as evil. Religion had them brainwashed and it did the same to me.

The divorce rate in this country has slightly declined. This is not because people are more committed, but less likely to marry. Unwed unions are increasing. Commitment to anything seems like a thing of the past. It looks like the problem is getting worse. I hope this information helps people learn from our mistakes.

When it was obvious my first wife didn't love me and wouldn't return, I almost had a nervous breakdown. It was difficult to eat, sleep or work. People told me I looked bad; their sympathy didn't help. I asked God to analyze me as a professional psychiatrist would. I told Him, He was the smartest being in the universe, and I knew His advice was free. I told God I felt almost ready for a mental hospital. I knew He would tell me exactly what I needed. God's counsel is always perfect.

Instantly, I was having a day dream or vision. I saw myself lying on a psychiatrist's lounge. Someone was standing over me. His face was void or blurred. The man was God, speaking to me. He said, Tony, I am not going to evade the issue. I will get straight to the point. You have a serious problem. If you don't get rid of this problem, it will kill you. You know what it is; you are still in love with your wife. You need to let the marital love die and love her differently. The revelation from God made me sad, but it gave me hope that I could survive, somehow.

I had strange thoughts a few months after my wife asked, "Can't you get it through your thick skull Tony, I don't love you anymore?" The sensation that came on me a few months later, made me feel guilty. The emotion caused me to have an attraction toward beautiful women. I didn't notice other women that way before. I had been a happily married man for over ten years.

Immediately, I realized it was normal for a man to feel this way. I decided before my thoughts became lust, I should ask God for a good looking Christian woman, with a son and daughter about my children's ages. My faith was strong enough to know—it was a done deal.

I was self-employed in the carpet cleaning business for over ten years. I began when I married my first wife. One day an insurance company asked me to look at a flooded carpet. The job was in the home of—you guessed it, Karen. She borrowed a vacuum and extracted the water, but I needed to look at it. My inspection shifted from the damp carpet, to the Christian mother with a son and daughter about my children's ages. Karen and I knew our marriages would end in divorce. We had physical and spiritual attractions toward each other. I believed it was God answering my prayers, and I'm sure of it now. We enjoyed talking about Jesus Christ and sharing our faith. Several years later, Karen told me she cried when I explained what Jesus meant to me. I didn't notice her tears as we talked about God.

Before I left her home, I made a bold statement. I said, "I would like to date you someday." She quickly replied, "I would like to date you; however, I have a problem." "What is that?" I asked. She said, "I have a boyfriend, but I don't really love him." I asked, "How long have you been dating him?" She said, "About three months." I asked, "How long have you known that you don't love him?" She replied, "About three months." I asked her, "When are you going to listen to the Holy Spirit?" She dropped her head and blushed. She said, "I will take care of this problem." Karen did the right thing. Many people stay with someone they don't love. (not good)

Three weeks later, I called Karen. She stated, "I didn't think you were going to call." I explained that I didn't want to move too fast. In one way, it didn't seem right to cause a breakup, but in another way it did. We shouldn't date someone we don't love; we may end up in an unhappy marriage. Since she didn't love him, she should end it. We began dating and were married one year later.

We were members of a local Baptist church and went almost every service. The church was large and several preachers attended. One cold February night, a preacher taught a Bible study. He was an excellent teacher, except for some of his doctrines. There was an arrogance about him that didn't impress me. The preacher made fun of those who prayed in tongues. He spoke a gibberish that didn't sound like tongues to me. My wife was deeply offended. The Holy Ghost and praying in the Spirit was very important to Karen. Many share that sentiment.

Karen declared, "I will never go back to that church." She wanted a church that taught the full gospel. There were full gospel churches around, but I was troubled by her reaction. I began to study the baptism of the Holy Ghost. After receiving this, I didn't understand why it was so important to her.

We visited many non-denominational churches. We attended some for several weeks. At others, once or twice was enough for Karen. Perhaps she was searching for the perfect church. There is none. It's true; some are better than others. We can overlook slight mistakes and gain the good. Many don't go to church; it's difficult to find a good one!

I began to lose interest in her religion. Eventually, no style of religion impressed me. Karen and the full gospel churches were persuasive. They convinced me other churches fell short in teaching the Gospel of Jesus Christ. For many years, I was disgusted with any religion. It seemed they all deviated from the truth.

I was saddened, and withdrew into myself. I was aware of the two main commandments; love God and love people. I knew scriptures well. Psalm 119:11 was constantly with me. "Thy word have I hid in mine heart, that I might not sin against thee." Where I went wrong was not studying and doing what it said.

Karen played tapes of preachers and spiritual music. The TV was almost always on something spiritual. She had a large collection of videos, tapes, and books. She wouldn't watch anything denominational. The material was charismatic or full gospel. She preferred the Holy Ghost and—signs and wonders. For years, I tried to accept Karen's religion. My heart wasn't in it, or right with God. I drifted through life without having the love, peace and happiness I desired. If I had studied God's Word as He instructs, things I needed would have been provided. When we seek God's kingdom first and what is right, God gives us what we need. I'm interpreting Mt. 6:33.

We rarely viewed TV together. Karen went to the recreational room, watched television or listened to the radio and tapes. Sometimes she viewed secular programs. She wanted closer to God but was influenced by the wrong crowd in a negative way.

Large windows overlooked our pool. Karen found the room restful. Outside speakers filled the pool area with music. The pool was larger than most, twenty by forty feet. The concrete section around the pool was large. We entertained family and friends. Sometimes, we had forty to fifty people in our home. Karen enjoyed her guests. She was respectful of others, and careful to not offend with the full gospel. She played praise and worship music, and mixed in something patriotic.

Karen was also political. She agreed with fundamental Christians and conservative political viewpoints. Karen supported many organizations with monthly donations. She joined the National Rifle Association (NRA) and didn't own a gun. I've always respected a person who was steadfast in their convictions. We agreed on most everything, except certain spiritual matters. It was a division between us.

We should be compatible before we marry, especially on spiritual matters. Karen was honest about her spiritual beliefs, before we became too serious. Spiritual differences caused me no concern. She addressed issues involving the children. I assumed we could handle any problem, with God's help. He was always there to assist and would have done more, if we had allowed it. Our problems were our fault—not God's. I was actually blind to any conflicts, because all I could see—was a good looking Christian mom, with a boy and girl about my children's ages. She was God's answer to my prayer; I didn't foresee any problems.

Talk about naive; I won the first place award. I should've known we would have troubles. "These things I have spoken unto you, that in me ye might have peace. In the world ye shall have tribulation: but be of good cheer; I have overcome the world." (John 16:33) Everyone has problems. Jesus helps us overcome if we do what He instructs. I've noticed a common thing in religions: People don't follow their own Bible. I've been guilty.

Karen and I were using the wrong kind of love to establish a relationship. Instead of using God's love that is all knowing, powerful and wise called agape love, we were using another love. Describing God's love would go on forever, because God is forever. Everyone struggles with the deep things of God.

It's obvious, what type of love was guiding my reasoning. Eros love or the romantic type of love was influencing my decisions. This kind of love works for romance, creating a bond, intimacy and pleasure in a marriage. Eros love doesn't resolve financial matters and differences.

We need God's kind of love. With Eros love guiding a couple, the sin of fornication can follow quickly. I'm sorry to admit, we did this. Problems that should've been resolved, were forgotten or ignored. Christians commit this sin and suffer later in life. "Be not deceived; God is not mocked: for whatsoever a man soweth, that shall he also reap." (Gal 6:7) There are consequences to actions. Remember, if we ask God to forgive us, He will if we stop. Repent means stop and change.

A few years into our marriage, I began having lower back problems. Friends that helped in my business told me to slow down. They said, "You are working too hard. Why don't you get a job with us and do the carpet cleaning on your days off?" I didn't listen because, I thought I was tough. Sometimes, we think we're self sufficient and can handle anything on our own; that is wrong.

The job was manufacturing cable for the television industry. I didn't think about my friend's suggestion, until my back problems made me consider it. The work schedule was four days on with four days off, and a work day was twelve hours. I thought, I could do the cleaning on my days off and go full-time again when my back was better.

I took the job and stayed for twelve and a half years. Eventually, I returned full-time to carpet cleaning. During that thirteen year period, I became obsessed with: whitewater rafting, and kayaking. My passion for safety escalated, since I was the river guide. I spent thousands of dollars toward a patent on a rescue knife invention. Eventually, I gave up, but I made sure no one could patent my design. I hope someday to get my knife in production. My obsessions were different than Karen's. She went to church, religious conventions, and prayer meetings. I focused on work and play.

Karen's church was beginning to literally, get on my nerves. All I heard was Holy Ghost, speak in tongues and healing. These teachings shouldn't be our main focus. The Gospel of Jesus Christ contains much more. Karen found a church that was anything but full gospel. Karen asked me if she could donate one thousand dollars to this church. I said, "Sure, I think that's a great idea." She didn't hear my sarcasm, and wrote the check. I knew the donation would deplete our account, or close to it. I was frustrated and didn't care that we were almost broke.

9

Soon after that, my casual drinking increased. My nerves were shattered and my hair began disappearing from the left side of my head. Three inches above my left ear was bald. I was able to comb my hair over it, so no one knew. I dealt with stress before, but not like this. We should've communicated more. When elders speak, listen. We have wisdom occasionally, even if we've learned it—in many difficult ways.

After getting drunk and totaling one of my vans, reality set in. I had problems that needed solving. A court order provided a counselor, to show me the way. He was a friend of mine, who gave me advice that I desperately needed. He asked me to read two books which helped me understand some things. I was resolving my problems, calming down and getting better. Even my hair was returning to normal.

I begged Karen to show more love and affection. She stated, "My mother rarely told me, I love you, but I know she did." I probably fell short in expressing my love. While attempting a Bible study, I didn't get anywhere. Karen said, "You are the one who has all the problems, and someone who doesn't attend church or study their Bible, won't teach me anything." I understood her rebuke, and was deeply troubled. Happiness seemed beyond my grasp.

Point Well Taken—It Gets Progressively Worse

I developed another problem. The lust I had years before, resurfaced. Then, it was lust causing me to commit the sin of fornication. Later, it was influencing me to commit adultery. Jesus declared this, "But I say unto you, That whosoever looketh on a woman to lust after her hath committed adultery with her already in his heart." (Mt. 5:28) My ugly act didn't go all the way, but the lust had turned into adultery. Lust of the flesh involves more than sexual desires. We can lust after things, money, or selfish pride. "For all that is in the world, the lust of the flesh, and the lust of the eyes, and the pride of life, is not of the Father, but is of the world. And the world passeth away, and the lust thereof: but he that doeth the will of God abideth for ever." (1 John 2:16–17)

If sin isn't stopped, it gets progressively worse. Sin is promoted by the devil and his fallen angels. They are no longer angels; they are evil spirits. Many call them demons.

I see clearly, pride leads the way for other sins and is difficult to detect. It's a struggle for anyone, rich or poor. We must guard against this evil. We rid ourselves of pride with humility. Stay humble, or pride will humble and destroy; it's dangerous.

We have to change, stay in church, read the Bible and pray or face destruction. The Bible states, "For the wages of sin is death; but the gift of God is eternal life through Jesus Christ our Lord." (Rom. 6:23) We must develop self control. This is possibly the most difficult aspect of a Christian. In the flesh we do things that come natural. Walking in the Spirit helps us change and live different. We'll do things that promote life—not death. "For to be carnally minded is death; but to be spiritually minded is life and peace." (Rom. 8:6) Carnal means fleshly.

We should strive to walk in God's Spirit. It takes more than going to church. We must follow Jesus to the end of our lives. Be a doer of the Word and not a hearer only. Some study God's Word, know it well, but don't do it. "But be ye doers of the word, and not hearers only, deceiving your own selves." (James 1:22) Walking in the Spirit is doing God's Word and it's necessary. "And they that are Christ's have crucified the flesh with the affections and lusts. If we live in the Spirit, let us also walk in the Spirit. Let us not be desirous of vain glory, provoking one another, envying one another." (Gal. 5:24–26)

When wrong thoughts come, change the subject in your mind, by immediately thinking on good things. This is an excellent way to find peace and the elusive dream—happiness! "Finally, brethren, whatsoever things are true, whatsoever things are honest, whatsoever things are just, whatsoever things are pure, whatsoever things are lovely, whatsoever things are of good report; if there be any virtue, and if there be any praise, think on these things." Philippians 4:8 gives amazing peace! I'm certain thinking on good things, is crucial to overcoming evil.

Sin will hurt forever. I would always love Karen, even though she wouldn't forget my sin against her. Fornication can lead to worse sins. While many don't view this as sin, God's Word does. We shouldn't think since we're saved, our sins don't matter! What we think, say and do matters a great deal.

God forgives sin if we sincerely ask Him. We must not continue but repent—change and stop. Many people want Jesus as Savior without Him being Lord or King of their life. We cannot have Him as Savior without accepting Him as Lord. Some play games with Him, while they make the rules. Often, they find a church that teaches too-good-to-be-true doctrines. A bogus assurance of salvation is no assurance. False prophets teach a false sense of security. The only security is found in Jesus Christ. Make sure you are in Him and He is in you. We must overcome things if we want to enter heaven.

God won't forgive the unpardonable sin. Blaspheming the Holy Ghost is resisting His gift of salvation. If we speak against the Holy Spirit or Holy Ghost, we are in danger of committing the unpardonable sin. "And whosoever speaketh a word against the Son of man, it shall be forgiven him: but whosoever speaketh against the Holy Ghost, it shall not be forgiven him, neither in this world, neither in the world to come. Either make the tree good, and his fruit good; or else make the tree corrupt, and his fruit corrupt: for the tree is known by his fruit. O generation of vipers, how can ye, being evil, speak good things? for out of the abundance of the heart the mouth speaketh. A good man out of the good treasure of the heart bringeth forth good things: and an evil man out of the evil treasure bringeth forth evil things. But I say unto you, That every idle word that men shall speak, they shall give account thereof in the day of judgment. For by thy words thou shalt be justified, and by thy words thou shalt be condemned." (Mt. 12:32–37)

Justified means vindicated, made right, blameless and free from sin. I will quote verses later explaining how we aren't justified by the works of the law. We're justified by grace, faith, works of faith and words. Yes, it's important what we say and do. The main way we are justified is—by the blood of Jesus Christ! (paraphrasing Romans 5:9)

Some say; I don't curse or deny Him. Being indifferent to the King can lead to blasphemy. Jesus Christ is God and someone we must bow to, worship, honor and obey. If we want to make it to heaven, we will let Him lead the way.

If you feel like the direction you've chosen is leading you toward the unpardonable sin, please remember His grace is sufficient. God is good and His mercy endures forever. Jesus helps reverse the direction we're on, no matter how horrible it is. He loves us and He always will. God will never leave us, but we can leave Him. We can repent and come back to Him. Our Heavenly Father's will is—that none should perish and He said, Return, oh backsliding children... (paraphrasing 2 Peter 3:9 and Jeremiah 3:14)

Whosoever believes on the name of Jesus Christ will be saved. An intellectual acceptance and a head knowledge is not enough. The belief should be a genuine heart changing belief. Some pretend to believe and almost convince themselves they have salvation. Follow this story and you'll see with crystal clear persuasion that God's plan for salvation is expressed in a comprehensive manner. I've made it simple, so a young child can understand. Hopefully, older people who are set in their ways will see how false prophets have misconstrued the glorious Gospel of Jesus Christ. Just be teachable; I am. The last part of Proverbs 1:7 tells us—fools despise wisdom and instruction.

If you feel I've made any wrong statements so far, please stay with this story. You'll see scriptures in later chapters that support the things I write. The story is incredible and more than bizarre at times. The inspiration of the Holy Spirit is the best part and His Word is most inspiring. I welcome correction, instruction, Bible study and will always remain teachable. No one knows everything, and some spiritual concepts won't be understood until we get to heaven. We mortals struggle with the deep things of God, but soon He will change us to immortality. *Father please show us the truth and nothing else. Help us to love you and people. Help us follow and obey you to the end of our lives or until you come and take us home to heaven. I ask in the name of Jesus Christ, the name above all names.*

CHAPTER TWO

THE SEARCH FOR THE CHURCH

K aren and her friends were determined to establish a full gospel or word church. I asked her, "What is a word church?" She stated, "A word church teaches the fullness of the gospel." I declared, "Karen, if the other churches in this county aren't teaching from the Word of God, what book are they using?" She was unaware that some denominations teach properly.

We must rightly divide the Bible to get an accurate interpretation. Comparing scriptures helps us live by every word, like Jesus taught. Verses taken out of context create false doctrines. Karen said, "If we leave out teachings like tongues, healing or anything, we may give up our salvation and if we add to the words, plagues will come on us."

These cautions are written at the end of the Bible in Revelation. I'll discuss these in detail near the end of this story. If you think the statement, once saved—always saved, will be determined, perhaps it will. With God's help, I can take this journey and go deeper than I thought possible. We can do all things through Christ.

I didn't understand then, but I see clearly now; Karen struggled with comparing scriptures; so did I. This is how we rightly divide God's Word, "comparing spiritual things with spiritual." (last part of 1 Cor. 2:13) I believe everyone struggles, with interpreting the Bible. Thank God, we have humble pastors, who serve others and lead rather than rule. These preachers rarely lead people astray.

It's clear, Karen didn't take away from God's Word. However, she was taught to add to the words. That can lead to an early departure from this life, by causing a plague.

This story is strange and unrealistic at times. It took a long time to put the puzzle together. If I hadn't found a church that was like family, I may not have survived. The Spirit of God in them, helped me. "Greater love hath no man than this, that a man lay down his life for his friends." (John. 15:13) I would lay down my life for them, or give my life as a living sacrifice. "...ye present your bodies a living sacrifice, holy, acceptable unto God which is your reasonable service." We find this in Romans 12:1. This is the last part of the verse.

They Were Looking For The Impossible

The handful of women who searched for the perfect church, failed to realize they were looking for the impossible. A church that consists of imperfect people will inevitably make mistakes.

God placed the treasure of His Holy Spirit inside earthen vessels, that the excellence of the power may be from God, and not from us. (2 Cor. 3:5) "Not that we are sufficient of ourselves to think anything as of ourselves; but our sufficiency is of God." We must remain humble or we'll be humbled, and it's embarrassing. I know this from experience. The wrong kind of pride is deadly and difficult to detect.

The ladies were searching for—what they already had. All those things were accomplished by Jesus Christ on the cross at Calvary. We should receive the signs, wonders, miracles and healings, and not try to produce them. Full gospel people add to the words of the Bible and criticize others for taking away from the words. Division in the body of Christ should come to an end.

Jesus asked this odd question, "Suppose ye that I am come to give peace on earth? I tell you, Nay; but rather division:" (Luke 12:51) Jesus caused division between the righteous and unrighteous. This separation was necessary so we would see the need for salvation. Jesus wanted to eliminate the lukewarm. He wanted people to commit to Him and stop the confusion. Confusion is from the devil, and should be eliminated. Lukewarm will be addressed in another chapter.

Jesus, by no means, wanted division between Christians. We are His family. God protects His own, and prepared a place for us in heaven. Hell was prepared for the devil and his angels. However, if we don't choose to follow Jesus, we follow the devil and evil spirits into the place of torment.

Let's come together, all religions, and be of one mind and one accord. Isn't being born-again and spending forever in heaven the main thing? Perhaps a revival will spread over the world.

The ladies pursued their agenda with passion. They loved God intensely, so they thought. Something was wrong with their attempt to build a full gospel church. Their efforts continued for twenty years or more with no success. Perhaps some of these women had unforgiveness, or struggled with expressing love. Why did their efforts fail? Could we guess wrong motives or unsound doctrines? Maybe all applied.

The ladies followed preachers who graduated from a certain Bible college in the Midwest. Preachers from that college came to our town and taught once a week. They hoped the Bible study would grow into a church. I was apprehensive of them; they added to the words of the Bible. They misused spiritual gifts by entertaining people.

When we seek power, glory, signs, wonders and miracles, we'll get prideful. Evil spirits confuse and eventually destroy. Seek His glory properly and He will help overcome evil. A dozen or more men tried to establish a church. I decided if something worked, I could join later. All these churches stayed small, and didn't last long. Looking back, I see why they failed.

A preacher and his wife started a church in their home. They graduated from the same college as the others. This couple was an inspiration to me. They knew how to walk in love. The man met the qualifications of a pastor. They were sweet, kind, and soft spoken. The church didn't last long. People got in the way. Eventually, the man and his wife realized the Bible college was wrong. I heard from someone else, they were embarrassed to admit where they attended school. The couple united with a good church later. *Father, I ask you to bless that couple and their family in the name of Jesus Christ.*

Thank God, He chastises or disciplines me. The Bible explains, we wouldn't be His, but illegitimate, without chastisement. He let me know; I was doing things without asking for His help. As usual, I got things backwards. He wants to assist in everything. I sincerely asked Him to forgive me. I told my Father I was coming back as His little child.

Jesus teaches, "...Verily I say unto you, Whosoever shall not receive the kingdom of God as a little child, he shall not enter therein." (Mark 10:15) It doesn't matter how old we are; we must acknowledge God as our Father in heaven. This helps eliminate pride. We haven't arrived in our spirituality. Let him who thinks he stands, take heed or he will fall.

When we take on the difficult mission of judging, as I'm doing by writing this, we must rebuke with a spirit of meekness, kindness, and love. I will continue to do this. My objective is to help others as I seek truth, healing and forgiveness. I'm willing to confess my faults. I hope others do the same, and we can draw closer to our Heavenly Father. We confess to people we trust; we shouldn't confess to some! Only God should hear some confessions.

Karen was excited about a young preacher. It seemed like a church was forming. She was convincing about his talents and got me interested; I began attending. The preacher had a positive message and the church grew quickly. He moved to Taylorsville and we cleaned their home at no charge. We gave—sometimes to a fault.

People were enthusiastic about our new church. Even though it grew fast, it only lasted a few months. A serious problem caused the small church to close. The preacher was committing the sin of adultery. He had a girlfriend before he started the church, and it was an ongoing affair. Our congregation was devastated. Most of them had been hurt in churches before. Karen was sad and deeply hurt. The preacher should have known, the Bible says we can't hide sin.

Karen was angry, because no one consulted with her. She said, the preacher should repent, ask for forgiveness, everyone forgive, and the church continue. Remember the expression, easier said than done? We have to forgive, but at times a man loses the right to preach. There are guidelines for pastors and deacons in the Bible.

Karen failed to realize the pastor's wife was devastated. It would take her a long time to heal, if she ever could. Karen didn't heal. This hurt added to a long list of hurts, and there were more to come.

Preachers know the qualifications of a pastor. He missed one by a mile. A pastor should be above reproach. Preachers are held to a higher standard. Those who are called the men of God must beware. "For unto whomsoever much is given, of him shall be much required." (Luke 12:48) Teachers and preachers, should remember this caution. (James 3:1) "My brethren, be not many masters, knowing that we shall receive the greater condemnation." James was referring to teachers and himself. Don't be so quick to teach; it's a responsibility with a stricter judgment.

This scripture means teachers can condemn themselves. Other people will condemn them also. So far as God's judgment being worse, perhaps it won't, if they're judged at the believers' judgment for saved people. However, if they are judged at God's great white throne, it is worse. We must study and teach God's truth. "It is a fearful thing to fall into the hands of the living God." (Heb. 10:31) We shouldn't have a spirit of fear, but we must fear God.

Karen was resilient and didn't want anyone to see her hurting. She thought her hurts were hidden and God would heal them. Sometimes, we overestimate the strength of our faith and fail to recognize stress. This was the road Karen was on. Like me, she had a pride problem. It will not only humble a person, it can kill. When sickness came on Karen, she was in denial. I admired her faith, but begged her to take medicine or see a doctor. I struggled with the same problem.

God heals in many ways. Sometimes, He uses a doctor, hospital or medicine. The Bible tells us, "Every good gift and every perfect gift is from above, and cometh down from the Father of lights..." (James 1:17)

18

Whatever method heals us, we should be thankful to God. Give Him the credit, glory, honor and respect He deserves. Often, we take credit for things we shouldn't and forget—we can't do anything without Him.

Karen is healed and happy in heaven. I have comfort knowing she is in good hands. To know Jesus as your Savior is comforting. We are confident someday we'll hear, well done good and faithful servant and not, depart from me, you that work iniquity. We can't overcome iniquity or sin on our own. Only Jesus Christ and His precious blood will cleanse us from all unrighteousness. We follow Him, because we have to, if we want eternal life in heaven. When we sin, He is faithful to forgive, if we sincerely ask Him and stop doing it!

CHAPTER THREE

THE MOTHER PROBLEM

I was close to my mother. We traveled almost everywhere together. Karen really loved her too, and wanted mom on our vacations almost every time, even on short trips.

Karen loved everybody and there was no doubt she was a Christian. Mother was the same. Since Karen didn't know my father well, she became close to mom. My father died of heart problems soon after I began dating Karen. Father was a good judge of character and said this about Karen. "That lady has class."

I Had The Problem

I didn't mean to imply my mother was a problem. I had the problem of being too close. When people backed out on a white water river trip, she and I went anyway. We both enjoyed the company of people and had more fun when we shared trips with others. If I wanted to kayak a river, my mom went along for the ride. At times, she got lost trying to find the take out, even with my homemade maps. When I needed a shuttle service, she was always available.

I'll never forget one cool winter day, mom and I flipped a raft in the first rapid on the Nantahala River. The water was higher than normal. Two days before, a warm front came from the south and saturated the canyon.

It was close to spring, about the middle of March. The Nantahala Gorge in North Carolina is famous and—cold.

We wore wet suits, dry suits, splash gear and gloves. I was properly organized for problems, but didn't expect it. Mother didn't listen to my safety instructions on the way to the river. She hadn't experienced trouble on a river before. She didn't expect anything but a good time; however, things happen on a river.

I hoped to instill in mom a method of self rescue on whitewater. All whitewater paddlers should know how to take care of themselves. There was a possibility, I wouldn't be in a position to assist mom. She might be on her own, swimming a wild river at high water. Mother might have to rescue herself. She had experience, but I remained concerned.

Soon after the flip, I found mother under the raft. After pulling the raft off her, I shouted, "Swim toward the island." It was a perfect place to recover from the upset. However, mom missed the opportunity. She was backstroking, looking straight up and swimming the wrong direction.

I stayed on course for the island. When I was close and the water became shallow enough to avoid foot entrapment, I planted my feet at a forty-five degree angle and contacted the rocky river bed safely. A foot entrapment could kill me. I knew without my help, mom might perish in the next set of long and powerful rapids. Time was of the essence. My mother encountered fast water on the left of the island. I entered slow current in front of the island. After standing in shallow water, I flipped the raft right side up and jumped in. The tiny raft flipped again. Panic is the emotion that must be avoided in a river rescue. In a situation like this, calm is the key. As my frustration increased, I intensely refocused my efforts and made an attempt, that was successful.

Using a kayak paddle with the small raft, I caught up to mom quickly. Suddenly, a boater and his wife came running down the river bank. The man had a professional throw rope. I lifted my left arm to initiate the throw; his heroic attempt was unsuccessful. People definitely need to practice rope throws under duress. It could save someone's life.

When that attempt failed, I knew it was up to me. I glanced around for eddies (calm waters) and didn't see any. There was nothing but fast water, and it was headed for huge waves. Mother was doing a good job holding the perimeter line on the raft, but she was still in jeopardy. It was only a matter of time before hypothermia would cause mom to lose her grip on the rope.

I grabbed mom with my left hand, as I snagged a huge tree branch. An excruciating pain went through my right bicep. I held the tree and pulled mother into the raft; it worked. We negotiated the rapids to perfection, caught an eddy on river left, and took a break. I asked mom why she was looking up and not looking downstream. She said with a big smile, "I was praying, and I knew you would save me."

The couple who tried to rescue us came jogging down a path toward us. They were concerned and the man explained what my problems were. He said the front of the raft was too high, and it needed balancing. His wife declared, "You hit the big waves perfectly, but your raft pulled a wheelie all the way over." I was somewhat shaken, but still considering how to balance the small boat.

I said, "Well, I suppose mother and I will probably call it a day." Mom said, "No! If you get the boat balanced, I want to run the rest of the river." We balanced the raft and ran the Nantahala in style. Mother and I loved every minute of it! The real test of a river guide is performing under pressure and making sure rescues are successful.

When we got back to Taylorsville, mother made sure people in town heard how cruel I was to her. Her wonderful sense of humor always spiced up the stories of our river trips. The next Christmas, we paddled a larger raft down the French Broad River about thirty miles north of Asheville, N.C. We enjoyed a beautiful sunny day, relatively warm air, and a glorious time together.

Mother acted upset when I wouldn't invite her on big world class rivers. They contain ten foot waves, many hazards and powerful rapids rated class five. A class five rating is the highest level anyone in their right mind should attempt to navigate. I don't believe mom wanted to do those big rivers. However, she would have if I had suggested it. She trusted me and—oh how she loved the rivers!

Mother rafted two more whitewater trips on the Big Pigeon River in Tennessee, and one or two on the French Broad. She was in her early seventies, and something ugly was growing inside her liver. We hoped breast cancer from several years before was in remission, but it spread to her liver, without us knowing. While unaware of any problems mother might have, another one was headed her way.

A woman from another county befriended mother. She moved in with her, because mom was lonely. She pretended to have nursing experience, but mom didn't need help. My brothers and I didn't know at the time, she had health problems. The idea of her having a close friend seemed good and we hoped the live-in nurse would be a benefit.

The woman seemed nice, but we were suspicious. Years before, our father was the sheriff of our county. My oldest brother was also an officer. We started doing some detective work. What we discovered was shocking! The older woman had a long criminal record, and had stolen mother's identity. If I didn't have obsessive compulsive disorder (OCD) I had it now. With my brother's help, we went after that woman with a passion. With a Power of Attorney and a determined resolve, I remained involved in my mother's life much to the detriment of Karen and me.

Karen really loved me, to tolerate my obsessions. I was on a long mission to clean and remodel mother's house, so I could sell it. Then I bought a mobile home for her, and placed it on twenty acres of land she owned on a mountain. I could have paid myself out of mom's proceeds for the time I spent on these tasks. I chose to absorb the losses so mom could have more. My brothers and sister would also benefit, in the event mother died. I wanted to avoid strife in the family.

There wasn't enough time to complete mother's projects. I decided to quit my job at the cable company and continue carpet cleaning. Instead of focusing on my business, I gave mother most of my attention. Her projects were more time consuming than I expected.

Karen and I lived off my 401K and a home equity loan. It didn't bother me that I gave up my insurance. I thought when my business improved, I would purchase what we needed. Being optimistic is good if it's balanced with reality. Confidence motivating is great if we keep everything in balance. Optimism driven by a misguided religion is bad.

We had a pastor declaring, we could have anything we asked for. His positive attitude went beyond reality. He was so charismatic, people seemed under his control. The preacher was highly educated and could really produce a show. He brought in two evangelists, supposedly gifted with signs, wonders and miracles.

The preachers preferred signs, wonders and easy healings, ones that could be faked if necessary. Karen thought it was the power of God, and so did I for a while. We endured things I wouldn't wish on anyone. I accepted the religion because I loved Karen and wanted to please her. There are people who do well in full gospel ministries. Others get out of control. Of course any religion can be misguided and many are, in different ways.

Everything for mom turned out fine, but she only enjoyed her new home about one year. The super anointed preachers couldn't heal her liver cancer. The Lord helped mom make a peaceful transition to her permanent home in heaven. My wife Karen died two years later, and as I recall, none of the preachers came to the hospital to pray for her.

Let me backup a year or two before mother died. A young preacher came to town at the request of the spiritual ladies. He taught a Bible study which eventually became a church. The new church grew quicker, got larger, and lasted longer than the other word churches. We should keep our guard up, when it pertains to any religion. I've learned this the hard way. Churches should follow the Bible. What the church did was kill, steal and destroy.

Get ready to enter a world where evil spirits abound. We were subjected to things I wouldn't want anyone to experience. The worst part about demonic activity is—it's cleverly disguised. Many things done in the name of Jesus, are wrong. Beware of the horrendous things false prophets do; they use religion for financial gain.

CHAPTER FOUR

A NEW KID IN TOWN

This new preacher and his wife graduated from the same Bible college as the others. They had two beautiful children, a son a few years old and a younger daughter. The man became our pastor, and his wife, the praise and worship leader. This was their first church, so far as I know. Their next church may succeed, if they learn from their mistakes.

Once the women interviewed him, they rented a building and began the Bible study. The Bible studies continued for several months, before he started a church. He made it obvious many times over the next two years, it was his church. No one should own a church. I don't know if the man had ownership or not; he sure acted like it. Most churches have a system where one person isn't in total control; that is good. At our church there was one man in control, our pastor. I believe the Bible should always be our guide in everything. Look in Ephesians 5:23; it explains, Jesus Christ is the head of the church.

A pastor is the leader and should—take care of the church. He must lead with love. A former pastor of mine explained, it's easier to lead sheep than drive them. The Bible instructs leaders to not threaten people and show partiality. When a pastor uses favoritism with some of his members, his love walk is compromised. His expressions of love are contradicted by actions, it becomes hypocrisy!

In lowliness of mind, let each esteem others better or greater than themselves. (paraphrasing Phil. 2:3) We should seek counsel from our elders. In a multitude of counsel there is safety. People respect pastors more, if they walk in love with humility.

Karen convinced me to attend a Bible study, before the church was formed. It was close to the last Bible study, when I began attending. I was fascinated with the preacher's knowledge of God's Word. He found an excellent balance between preaching and teaching. I can't recall meeting anyone with a positive attitude like his. Being an optimist myself, I had high hopes for this church. I was overoptimistic and I've been guilty of that many times.

I told the preacher, I was willing to help. I stated, "I'm willing to help build this church, but I don't want any titles. I don't desire a deacon's position; I only want a place to attend church. When someone younger comes along with a desire to do things for God, I will gladly step aside and let them have my positions." The man didn't want any deacons. He heard stories of how they controlled pastors. He wanted the opposite. Eventually it was obvious; he controlled the church.

I'll Never Forget The Look The Preacher Gave Me

Years later, we can look back and see what was meant by a certain look or body language. I'll never forget the look the preacher gave me after I stated, "I'm willing to help build this church, but I don't want any titles." The look was; you will do what I say. Later, an evangelist friend of his, made this clear in a sermon on submission.

The man's sermon went like this: You should do whatever your pastor tells you. If he instructs you how to act, you should act that way. If he tells you how to talk, you should talk that way. If he informs you to dress a certain way, you should dress that way. If you want to submit to God, you must submit to your pastor. Never speak against him, even if he is wrong. I was shocked! Occasionally, I glanced at my pastor to see if he approved of the mean sermon. I could tell by his body language he was well pleased. I'm getting ahead of myself. It takes constant brain-washing for people to accept that teaching. It sounded like the wrong kind of control to me. Christians overlook way too much.

I didn't mean any disrespect with this chapter title. A new kid in town, was only a figure of speech. My pastor was in his early thirties. I was about fifty-one. Karen declared, "He could be my son." I felt the same, but we didn't act that way. We loved and respected him.

Services were Sunday morning, Wednesday night and occasionally, Sunday night. Karen and another lady taught healing on Tuesday and Thursday mornings. Healing was an important part of our church. Our pastor hoped the healing services would expand, to every day of the week. The pastor said, the church would move to a large tract of land with a new facility. Supposedly, God had shown him where the location would be. It seemed an excellent place for our new church.

The preacher thought we would purchase the 20,000 sq. ft. building we were currently in. He said half the building would be the youth center. The other half would be a healing center. Hospital beds would be provided. Prayer warriors would pray for people from all over the world. They would travel to Taylorsville, N.C. because of God's healing power. His power is everywhere. They'll figure it out.

Ten years before, a man came to town and taught a Bible study. He gave a prophecy that foretold of Taylorsville being this healing place. Other local churches were excited about this; they hoped their church would fulfill the prophecy.

All prophecies aren't from God. Look in 1 Corinthians 13:8. "Charity never faileth: but whether there be prophecies, they shall fail..." (1 Cor. 13:13) "And now abideth faith, hope, charity, these three; but the greatest of these is charity." Charity means love. It's amazing how some place faith and hope above love. God is love.

Some deny Jesus Christ is divine, or God. When they do this, they have become anti Christ. "Whosoever transgresseth, and abideth not in the doctrine of Christ, hath not God. He that abideth in the doctrine of Christ, he hath both the Father and the Son." (2 John 1:9) Whoever sins and doesn't stay in the teachings of Jesus doesn't have God. Whoever abides, or remains, in the teachings of Jesus has the Father and His Son.

We can't have God the Father, if we continue to deny Jesus Christ is the Son of God or that He is God. "...And we know that the Son of God is come, and hath given us an understanding, that we may know Him that is true, and we are in Him that is true, even in His Son Jesus Christ. This is the true God, and eternal life." (1 John 5:20)

Some have a head knowledge, but not a heart changing belief in Him. Repent and born-again means change; we become different. "Therefore if any man be in Christ, he is a new creature: old things are passed away; behold, all things are become new." (2 Cor. 5:17)

If a religion teaches Jesus Christ is the Son of God—but He is not God—it's wrong. Some won't consider Jesus Christ is God who came in the flesh. This is called, the spirit of antichrist. Many people aren't for Him; they are against Him or anti Christ. Relying on Jehovah God, our Heavenly Father, for salvation without Jesus Christ, will put us at the great white throne of judgment. We won't spend eternity in paradise or heaven, but the place of everlasting torment and pain. That place is called hell. Being separated from God, good people, and a marvelous brilliance beyond compare, would be painful. There will be sadness, of where our religion sent us. Don't be anti—Christ!

Beware of antichrist deceivers. "For many deceivers are entered into the world, who confess not that Jesus Christ is come in the flesh. This is a deceiver and an antichrist. Look to yourselves, that we lose not those things which we have wrought, but that we receive a full reward. Whosoever transgresseth, and abideth not in the doctrine of Christ, hath not God. He that abideth in the doctrine of Christ, he hath both the Father and the Son. If there come any unto you, and bring not this doctrine, receive him not into your house, neither bid him God speed: For he that biddeth him God speed is partaker of his evil deeds." (2 John 1:7–11) Don't let these people in your home and don't accept their religion. If you're in a religion that is against Jesus Christ, get out!

Don't follow the wrong crowd, regardless of who they are, or their title. Study different translations of the Bible. The King James Version is probably the most accurate, but the old English is difficult and we need modern translations. "...and in multitude of counselors there is safety." (Prov.24:6) Don't change the meaning of the old version. That is taking away from the words—a deadly mistake.

No Man Cometh Unto The Father But By Me...Jesus

Explaining scriptures with modern English, isn't taking away from the words, if we're paraphrasing or interpreting accurately. Some preachers criticize modern translations while they explain scriptures with modern English. This contradiction isn't necessary. Misinterpreting the King James Version is—taking away from the words.

Some people feel enlightened on certain subjects. I've been that way at times in my life. I hope others don't consider me a know-it-all. I'm not because—no one is! I teach only subjects I'm familiar with. In which case, I've given advice. I tried to give my pastor advice; it offended him. He resented it and viewed me as a threat.

I obeyed most of his rules and tried to please him. The main rule was be submissive to the pastor; refer to him as pastor, then his name. It makes me wonder about the Bible college he attended. Other preachers from the same school, viewed submission and titles the same way. Many preachers are prideful, esteem themselves better than others, show no love or humility and fall into condemnation.

Sometimes, I talked too fast and forgot to use his title. It really bothered my pastor. We had to submit to his wife. We had to submit to the women who taught healing and highly regard our head usher.

Our pastor declared we could say something against him, but nothing against his wife or children. It was difficult to believe him, because he contradicted himself often. He didn't like anyone advising him on anything. The preacher didn't mean it when he declared we could say something

29

against him. This was his first lie that I caught. He taught us to never speak against him. At that time, I didn't consider this a lie. He just misspoke; a preacher knows lying is dangerous. After two and a half years of bold faced lies, I questioned every time the man spoke.

A tape series on submission was produced by a preacher who graduated from the same college. These tapes must be listened to and it was mandatory if we were to become members. We should live a consistent Christian life. If we served in any leadership positions, we shouldn't smoke or drink alcohol. I confessed these faults to my pastor. He didn't like it, but he needed my help.

The Bible says, "Happy is he that condemneth not himself in that thing which he alloweth." (Rom. 14:22) If I considered something not right or wrong nor black or white, I thought of it as a gray area. "for whatsoever is not of faith, is sin." This is the last part of Romans 14:23. I thought—if I allowed something in moderation without feeling guilty, I could do it in faith and it would not be sin. There was something making me nervous. It became clear; my pastor was trying to control me.

My pastor didn't like how I dressed. He expected ushers to wear a coat, tie and dress pants. Casual dress at church is okay with me. Can you find a dress code for church? The Bible mentions dressing modest and it wasn't a dress code for church.

The head usher rebuked me about the way I dressed. This was about two years after the church began. By this time, the pastor and I had been through several difficult moments. The man lied many times, screamed at me and made threats. You will see; I tolerated him more than I should have. I was patient; it's one of the fruits or qualities of the Spirit.

The usher said our pastor would purchase matching coats and ties and leave them in a back room. Ushers would wear dress pants and nice shirts. We were told to arrive early and put on the coats and ties. I asked the usher, "Can you show us in the Bible, where we are to dress fancy? If you can't, we will consider this a tradition of men, and avoid it like the plague. Would you please tell the pastor, it would be a waste of church funds to purchase coats and ties, that would hang in the back room and collect dust?"

A serious problem developed near the end of our pastor's sermons. This is the most important time in a service, the invitation. It's when people make important decisions for their lives. The pastor's son became disruptive and his father struggled with the situation.

A pastor should rule his own house well. The Bible explains, if he doesn't rule his own house well, how can he take care of the church. In First Timothy chapter three, it doesn't say he rules the church. Jesus taught—he that is greatest among you shall be your servant! I'm paraphrasing Mt. 23:11. Mark 10:42–45 says—leaders should minister (serve) in the church, not rule or be ministered to. Rule your own house with love, but serve and lead in the church! Remember—kings and dictators rule.

The boy's bad behavior began to have a negative impact. The ladies asked me to speak to our pastor about this problem. They wouldn't dare rebuke him. I knew the rebuke would have to come from me and I would not enjoy it. I've wondered why the difficult jobs always came my way, and why I accepted them. It was almost as if they were afraid of our pastor. I thought maybe the problems would take care of themselves. We weren't so fortunate.

Another serious problem surfaced in his wife. I viewed her as greater than me. I knew she meant well. However, she was demanding, and struggled with confusion. Sometimes, the woman's speech slurred and she staggered, laughed uncontrollably and fell to the floor. We thought God was performing signs and wonders and she was drunk in the Spirit. They enjoyed acting this way and wanted the rest of us to do the same.

Often, it's walking in the flesh and emotionalism. After a long time, I got caught up in the same thing. In hindsight, I'm glad it happened, so others can learn from my experience and avoid the irrational behavior. It took a long time for me to realize it was wrong. When we do things to act more spiritual, that aren't in God's Word, we get into a realm of demonic activity that might destroy us. If the preacher's wife hasn't changed, I think she will; she has a good heart. The preacher said she was filled with the Spirit. I don't think so. It was the power of mind control, witchcraft and at times—walking in the flesh.

Our pastor rarely called the Spirit of God, the Holy Spirit. He referred to Him as the Holy Ghost. Either term is accurate; they are like the same, with different functions. He preferred to proclaim, the Holy Ghost with much emphasis. The Holy Ghost gives power, among other things. Our pastor focused on power, signs and wonders. Seeking power becomes addictive. Money, power and control can easily cause someone to go astray. When used properly, they are tremendous assets.

Jesus said, "Notwithstanding in this rejoice not, that the spirits are subject unto you; but rather rejoice because your names are written in heaven." (Luke 10:20) Jesus knew if we focused on the power He has given, we would get in trouble. We should be thankful He has given us eternal life in heaven, and try to avoid pride. The Bible declares, "Pride goeth before destruction, and an haughty spirit before a fall." (Prov. 16:18)

The first sin was committed by the devil, which was pride. If we commit that sin and don't repent, we'll be judged severely. A Christian is to express humility. It's a necessary quality. (See 1 Peter 5:5.)

Our pastor taught us how to fall. He said falling was the way to receive from God. Some already knew how to fall when the pastor laid hands on them. I didn't know what to think, so I observed carefully. In the end, it was clear what happened, emotions and flesh.

My duty was to stand behind people and catch them as they fell. It was difficult on my back, especially when someone was overweight, but I managed. The pastor didn't try to make me fall. Maybe his gift of discernment showed him it would be awhile, before I would fall at his command. If we're taught to fall, it's the power of suggestions, mind control, and seeking signs. "A wicked and adulterous generation seeketh after a sign; and there shall no sign be given unto it, but the sign of the prophet Jonah." (Mt. 16:4) Jesus was speaking to His disciples. He knows seeking signs is not good. If we paid attention, we would see His signs, wonders and miracles all the time.

I wasn't trying to rebel; I was confused. "For God is not the author of confusion..." (1 Cor. 14:33) The preacher was also confused. I pray for my former pastor to stop the nonsense. People who follow false prophets most likely, will end up in a serious predicament. They could spend the rest of eternity in the wrong place! The good news is—they can stop!

Pride is a horrible thing. Often words have more than one meaning. The right kind of pride is good. We should be proud of our spouses and children. We should be proud of Jesus. If you aren't proud of Him, you should ask for His forgiveness and salvation. Sinful pride is when we boast about God-given talents or blessings. Anyone can have a pride problem, rich or poor. Many struggle with pride and it's a constant fight between my flesh and spirit. When we think we have excelled, pride is not far away.

Before I explain these false signs, and healings, I must elaborate on the control problem. When someone tries to control another person, the part being controlled is the mind. The brain causes our body parts to move. For example, if I wanted a man to do something, I wouldn't speak to his legs, feet, arms and hands. I would speak directly to him. It would be his mind that controlled his body.

Preachers speak a lot of words. If they are good words supported with scriptures, we consider this a good influence. Actually, if words confirm scriptures, we say God spoke through the preacher. A wise preacher always prays before speaking, asking God for guidance. They know many will believe anything they say, and perhaps be lead astray.

There is a huge difference between a preacher who makes a simple mistake, than one who teaches a wrong doctrine. We should overlook slight mistakes without getting offended; we all make mistakes. Most of us have tried to excuse or justify sins. It's the most dangerous thing we could ever attempt! No one can justify or validate sin.

A false doctrine is heresy, a doctrine of evil spirits. Don't let anyone lead you into a disaster. They might mean well, but what good is that, if you both spend eternity in hell. We influence people and teach others by the life we live.

There is good and bad control. It's good to control small children. It is essential to control a society with laws and law enforcement. Often, we make demands when we shouldn't.

Many years ago, Karen tried to control me. I decided to appeal to her spiritual side. I said, "Karen, would you please reason with me? God is more powerful than us, but He doesn't force anyone to do His will. He uses His still, small voice. His Holy Spirit speaks to our spirit gently. Some call this our conscience. What gives us the right to force or control each other? We shouldn't unless one of us is dreadfully wrong, and that mistake will cause harm." I realized I was guilty of the same problem. When we judge, we're usually guilty of the same thing.

"Judge not that ye be not judged. For with what judgment ye judge, ye shall be judged: and with what measure ye mete, it shall be measured to you again. And why beholdest thou the mote that is in thy brother's eye, but considerest not the beam that is in thine own eye? Or how wilt thou say to thy brother, Let me pull out the mote out of thine eye; and, behold, a beam is in thine own eye. Thou hypocrite, first cast out the beam out of thine own eye; and then shalt thou see clearly to cast out the mote out of thy brother's eye." (Mt. 7:1–5) If we judge ourselves first, we see clearly how to judge others—in the right way.

We apologized for controlling each other. It is witchcraft; it's a work of the flesh. If we walked in His Spirit, we would love more and sin less. I've decided to not control someone unless it's absolutely necessary. People would be amazed at the difference this could make in their lives. Christians shouldn't be selfish; they must serve. Some are disrespectful to others and control them. Sometimes it's unobvious and doesn't appear wrong. It's horribly wrong. If you're being hurt with control, please get help. It's mind control and a simple form of brainwashing. Over an extended period of time, it causes destruction. In the natural, things of God seem irrational or backwards. Trust me; I've done it both ways. Most of my life I've done what is natural, walking in the flesh. Late in life, I'm learning to walk in the Spirit. *Thanks Lord for your sweet Spirit.*

Do you want a formula for success? "Therefore take no thought, saying, What shall we eat? or, What shall we drink? or, Wherewithal shall we be clothed? (For after all these things do the Gentiles seek:) for your Heavenly Father knoweth that ye have need of all these things. But seek ye first the kingdom of God, and His righteousness; and all these things shall be added unto you." (Mt. 6: 31–33)

Many struggle with the basic necessities of life: food, clothing and shelter. The best way to acquire what we need is—seek God and His righteousness. He takes care of us, even more when we follow and obey. We would rather be blessed and have everything we need, instead of striving and struggling? Put God first; it makes a big difference.

The best feeling we could have is—walking in harmony with the living God who created the universe. We can act and think like Him. Apostle Paul said, "For who hath known the mind of the Lord, that he may instruct Him? But we have the mind of Christ." (1 Cor. 2:16) We see His signs, wonders, miracles and healings—when we follow Him. Some prefer fake, phony and fall to the floor foolishness.

We had a strange visitor at church. The woman thought relatives put curses on her. From what she told us, she had a troubled past. We didn't know what to expect from her or when to expect it. She fell to the floor and her body shook so violently, her shoes flew off. At times, other things fell off. She moved in circles on the floor. This happened when the preacher prayed for her, and sometimes without anyone doing anything. The show was ugly and disrespectful. There was nothing good about these bizarre episodes. God was not glorified, and the lady wasn't helped in any way.

Our pastor revealed he was controlled by a former pastor. He confessed, that one of his pastors had cursed him. Do you think the same spirit in those other preachers got into our pastor? Was our young pastor acting out, what he was subjected to in the past? We can become like others, especially our pastor or teacher; be careful.

People hurt others with the same hurts they've experienced. Could it be caused by demons? Oh yes, it sure could. At times, it's a natural reaction in our flesh. If the supernatural is working in us, we are in the Spirit.

How would you react if you were walking in the flesh? If someone shouts at you, you shout back. They push; you push them. They slap; you slap them. They hit you with their fist; you punch them. They pick up a deadly weapon; you pick up whatever you can. When someone hurts anyone, the hurt is often returned. It's natural to do this. What stops this cycle of sin is surrendering to Jesus Christ. We must live a surrendered life and let Him be our Lord. When we walk in the Spirit with God, we read His Word and hide it in our heart.

Jesus explained the heart. "A good man out of the good treasure of his heart bringeth forth that which is good; and an evil man out of the evil treasure of his heart bringeth forth that which is evil: for of the abundance of the heart his mouth speaketh." (Luke 6:45)

A soft answer turns away wrath. We should turn the other cheek. We must not return evil for evil, but good for evil. "Therefore if thine enemy hunger, feed him; if he thirst, give him drink: for in so doing thou shalt heap coals of fire on his head." (Rom. 12:20) Being nice to anyone who is mean to us, exposes their evil and humbles them. It hurts them at first, but it can help if they have a change of heart. If they don't change, at least we did right.

We should always remember this. (Eph. 6:12) "...For we wrestle not against flesh and blood, but against principalities, against powers, against the rulers of the darkness of this world, against spiritual wickedness in high places." We need to love and forgive people.

If you're a single parent and have trouble in relationships, think about what causes this. You may be hurting people with the same hurts you've experienced. People you've dated, hurt you. You in turn hurt others. Sometimes wrong seems right and right seems wrong. We sure get things backwards at times. Sometimes we believe self defense is the way, when we need self denial and a forgiving attitude. Fill your heart with God's Word. Speak good things that are pure, lovely, just and true.

The next time you meet a Christian who walks in the Spirit, you won't accuse them of being strange. You might be different like the Bible instructs. It's possible you'll be compatible and find the love of your life. I think most people have this desire. We don't go about it the right way at times. We should trust the Lord; stay close to Him and wait on Him to give us exactly what we need—His will. Remember, lean not to your own understanding.

The Bible teaches, don't be unequally yoked. Couples manage better if they have things in common. People enjoy being together, because of similar likes and dislikes. We need to understand each other long before committing to an intimate relationship. The best way to love, is focus on others instead of ourselves. True love like this will bless you.

Please, walk in the Spirit, or you may hurt another person you have a relationship with—your child. You don't want your children having trouble in relationships, especially with you. Children have enough peer pressure, without being provoked to wrath. Why don't you use the nurture and admonition of the Lord? The difference you'll see in your children could be amazing! His Word explains this in Eph. 6:4 and Colossians 3:21.

"Lay not up for yourselves treasures upon earth..." (Mt. 6:19) The next verse declares, "Lay up for yourselves treasures in heaven..." Verse twenty-one says, "For where your treasure is, there will your heart be also." We won't take our possessions to heaven. God has everything we'll need prepared for us. People will be treasures in heaven.

Be co-owners with Jesus of everything. "The Spirit itself beareth witness with our spirit, that we are the children of God: And if children, then heirs; heirs of God, and joint heirs with Christ; if so be that we suffer with Him, that we may be also glorified together." (Rom. 8:16–17) "He that overcometh shall inherit all things; and I will be his God, and he shall be my son." (Rev. 21:7) "And they overcame him by the blood of the Lamb, and by the word of their testimony; and they loved not their lives unto the death." (Rev. 12:11)

We overcome through our faith in Jesus Christ, the Lamb of God. It's by the cleansing power of His blood, grace and love, that we through faith overcome the devil and sin. In fact it's our faith that is counted for righteousness. This is found in Romans 4:5. Many misunderstand this and other parts of the Bible. They believe our works of faith has nothing to do with salvation. The works doctrine in conjunction with the salvation doctrine, will be covered in later chapters.

Many understand, that loving people is following Jesus. It takes the works of faith in Jesus Christ to accomplish this. Our works or bearing fruit isn't earning our salvation; it is the evidence of receiving God's free gift. Many don't grasp this concept and don't fully understand salvation.

It's my hope—that people have more assurance of their salvation. Some say it isn't our salvation; it's God's. When you accept and receive His free gift, it becomes yours. The Bible says, work out your own salvation with fear and trembling. Abide in Him; it means remain!

Selfishness has no place in a Christian. If we love money and things, we hate God. Jesus made this clear. "No man can serve two masters: for either he will hate the one, and love the other; or else he will hold to the one, and despise the other. Ye cannot serve God and mammon." (Mt. 6:24) Mammon is anything that we adore, worship or place before God. He said, "Thou shalt have no other gods before me." (Ex. 20:3)

The things we have are nice. It would be easy to overlook who gives them. Don't forget who owns everything, including us. "The earth is the Lord's, and the fullness thereof; the world, and they that dwell therein." (Psalm 24:1) It's possible people don't realize, they love possessions too much. God gives us plenty so we can help others. He expects us to love others the way he loves. "This is my commandment, That ye love one another, as I have loved you." (John 15:12) I always encourage people to begin studying in John. The fundamentals of God and love are there, and in John's three letters.

Some don't love their family as they should. They're selfish, and forget this scripture. "But if any provide not for his own, specially for those of his own house, he hath denied the faith, and is worse than an infidel." (1 Tim. 5:8) Please take care of your family; it sounds like we won't make it to heaven if we don't. How would you interpret that scripture?

Really good people can be deceived. If they love their possessions, they better change quickly. We might fool people, but God knows our hearts. We can't deceive Him because He knows our thoughts and intentions. "The Lord knoweth the thoughts of man, that they are vanity." (Ps 94:11) "...For the word of God is quick, and powerful, and sharper than any two edged sword, piercing even to the dividing asunder of soul and spirit, and of the joints and marrow, and is a discerner of the thoughts and the intents of the heart." (Heb. 4:12)

Jesus told His disciples how to abide in Him. Jesus said, "If ye keep my commandments, ye shall abide in my love; even as I have kept my Father's commandments, and abide in his love." (John. 15:10) Look at verse twelve once more. "This is my commandment, that ye love one another, as I have loved you." The key is—as I have loved you. We are to love as He loves. If we do, we'll abide or remain in Him.

This scripture is a conditional promise. "Blessed are they that do his commandments, that they may have right to the tree of life, and may enter in through the gates into the city." (Rev. 22:14) "Wherefore, my beloved, as ye have always obeyed, not as in my presence only, but now much more in my absence, work out your own salvation with fear and trembling..." (Phil. 2:12) Certain scriptures are simple and need no interpretation. If we think we don't have to do anything to get to heaven, we are sadly mistaken. I'll quote many scriptures that prove this fact. It's impossible to follow Jesus without the works of faith in Him.

True doctrines aren't as popular as false ones. This is exactly why people speak well of false prophets. False teachers extort fortunes from their followers. We're at fault, if we fail to study God's Word. It's high time to leave false teachers behind and focus on our Father's business. It is a must!

There is a doctrine that causes some to misinterpret a lot of God's Word. When you get to the end of this story, you'll see clearly how this doctrine has hurt, confused and misled others. I'm afraid many will miss heaven because of it. Please study and don't take my word for it; take God's Word. We have assurance of salvation by following His Word! Jesus made it plain; traditions can cause people to miss heaven.

A lie is often followed by more lies. When we tell a lie, we tend to tell more to cover it up. False teachings promote—more false teaching. When a doctrine is taught wrong, other scriptures are misinterpreted in an attempt to validate the teaching. Everything in God's Word lines up and doesn't contradict. We misinterpret when verses seem to contradict.

CHAPTER FIVE

THE HANDY MAN AND HIS FAMILY

A good man brought his family to our church. I got to know him well. It was obvious the man had a good heart. He had a hunger and thirst for righteousness. He loved everyone and his actions showed it.

The man couldn't have arrived at a better time. We were ready to move into the 5000 sq. ft. facility. The building needed a lot of work. The handy man owned a business; you guessed it, remodeling. While extremely talented, he could build almost anything. He worked for free on our church, in his spare time. He got his friends to do the same.

This gentleman was operating a ministry of helps, even though he struggled financially. The name he chose for his ministry was touching, The Father's Heart. The mission of the handyman was to feed and clothe needy people. He hoped to take the ministry to a higher level. The handy man managed the organization for over two years. He began it at his former church and was still operating the ministry on his own.

He thought he had a close relationship with our pastor. They shared the same vision and were determined to operate this ministry within our church. Many people began donating canned food and clothing.

The Father's Heart had helped people and was somewhat known in the community. After the pastor laid down his rules and made it clear this project would be his, the vision slowly died, but not with the handyman. The man politely told our pastor, God gave him the ministry, and he would operate it the way God led him. Trying to control others, will cause us to lose every time. Our pastor lost many opportunities.

While saddened, the good man continued to give. He told me, he was giving to God and not our pastor. The way he walked in love was a standard to follow. I believe the handy man and family will be blessed.

Our pastor viewed the man's wife as a problem. She wasn't being submissive to him. He couldn't get her to fall when he prayed for her. She didn't do fake things, or try to impress anyone. Eventually, the pastor didn't pray for her. The lady told me, she didn't want his prayers. She had a clear perception of his nonsense, but still helped with the remodeling. She was quiet in a virtuous way with a gift of discernment and a high degree of intelligence.

Our pastor called a meeting with the church leaders. We learned something that came as a shock. He stated there were three kinds of people in a church: sheep, goats and wolves. Sheep were good, but goats were stubborn and needed love to become good sheep. The third kind wolves, would never change. Since you couldn't change a wolf, you must get rid of it. He explained, the handyman's wife was a wolf. I didn't believe it but what could I do; he was in control of his church.

A pattern was developing. Anyone who didn't fully submit to our pastor was considered a problem. I didn't see this at first; I wasn't looking for faults in the preacher. Perhaps it was the blind leading the blind.

It's good when a preacher persuades people to do right. If he uses biblical principles, to convince us to change for the better, good for him. It's neither control nor manipulation. It is God's will. If we aren't doing the will of our Father in heaven we are in serious trouble. "Not everyone that saith unto me, Lord, Lord, shall enter into the kingdom of heaven; but he that doeth the will of my Father which is in heaven." (Mt. 7:21) We must do our Heavenly Father's will if we want to make it to heaven! That verse is easy to interpret.

Anything not done in love is in vain. Our preacher knew, he came on too strong at times. He wasn't tactful when a person needed constructive criticism. He asked me to handle problems, so he wouldn't be blamed if someone got upset. The most fundamental aspect of being a Christian was missed in all those college classes. I didn't go to college, but I know what love is.

The Bible teaches God is love. Explaining God is difficult; the same could be said for the God kind of love. If I understand anything, I hope it's love. 1 Corinthians 13 explains it well. "Charity suffereth long, and is kind; charity envieth not; charity vaunteth not itself, is not puffed up, Doth not behave itself unseemly, seeketh not her own, is not easily provoked, thinketh no evil; Rejoiceth not in iniquity, but rejoiceth in the truth; Beareth all things, believeth all things, hopeth all things, endureth all things." True love never fails. Charity means love and it is the most important attribute.

The Bible states this. "For if we would judge ourselves, we should not be judged." (1 Cor. 11:31) There is no need for someone to judge us if we have already done it. I have judged myself and will continue to do this. I fear only—my Heavenly Father's judgment.

Judge someone quickly if they are hurting your family. If a stranger came in your yard and was trying to kill your children, do you think it would be proper to judge them? It would be wrong to not judge them!

God has ordained authorities. Some have the title of judge. God's Word explains, we judge people and someday even angels when it's appropriate. Many think we shouldn't judge people and fail to realize, we have to. If we were considering a dangerous job, we might do a background check on someone. That is appropriate judging. You should judge me on what I write; please do it the right way. I'll quote many scriptures on the proper kinds of judging later. There are wrong and right ways to judge explained in the Bible.

In Mt. 5:44–46, Jesus made it plain. "But I say unto you, Love your enemies, bless them that curse you, do good to them that hate you, and pray for them which despitefully use you, and persecute you; That ye may be the children of your Father which is in heaven: for He maketh His sun to rise on the evil and on the good, and sendeth rain on the just and on the unjust. For if ye love them which love you, what reward have ye? Do not even the publicans the same?" Even sinners love people who love them. We have to love everyone, if we want to live in heaven. In the previous verse it's plain; we must love our enemies, bless them, do good to them, and pray for them, to be God's children. It's a tall order!

There are false prophets, and their followers, around us today. These people influenced Karen, in a negative way for over twenty years. This contributed to her early departure from this earth. This rebuke is meant to help false prophets because I love and forgive them.

Karen was only fifty-three. Do you think she made mistakes? Sure she did. Did I make mistakes? I have made numerous mistakes. I've confessed faults and will confess more. Our mistakes don't excuse others of theirs. Just because we make mistakes, it doesn't justify them. Some try to validate their sins. It can't be done. We must repent or—we shall all likewise perish. God loves us, and He is not willing that any should perish. Please don't be at the great white throne of judgment in shock and disbelief with multitudes of lost people. Repentance is a very good thing, and necessary!

Do you think we should stop false preachers from hurting others mentally, physically and of course the worst way—spiritually? In other words, preachers or anyone should stop destroying people. Before you get to the end of this story, you'll see how the devil uses people.

The handy man enjoyed the evangelist our pastor chose for a revival. We didn't realize he would become so problematic. We thought the man had a special anointing. As you will see, intelligent people are deceived, even Christians. People were manipulated, and hurt in many ways. I'll expose their fake tricks. Of course, the evangelist thought it was the power of God, and so did we for awhile. Please learn from our mistakes. You or someone you love may be in jeopardy!

Our pastor and his evangelist friend graduated from the same Bible college. He contacted the evangelist about a revival and the invitation was accepted. Everyone had high expectations and anticipated a good time.

Our pastor warned us that his friend got wild as he preached. He said the man prayed, sang, danced and ran in the Spirit. He informed us, the preacher wouldn't be happy unless he had everyone slain in the Spirit. He meant lying on the floor. Trying to display our notable spiritual traits opens the door for evil spirits.

Our pastor said signs, wonders and miracles would occur because the power of God would be present. He believed his friend had a strong anointing from God. He said the preacher was so gifted, he could look at someone, and give them insight into their future. (word of knowledge) This gift is good if not misused; we saw it misused!

He told ushers to move fast, because the man moved quickly laying hands on people. Perhaps he worried about a lawsuit as people would fall to the concrete floor. It had a floor covering, but the impact would be almost the same as hitting concrete. Each night's attendance averaged thirty people. There was a definite method to the madness which ensued. It took a long time to see clearly that evil was disguised as good.

The preacher prayed in tongues, usually without interpretation. He sang in tongues. He had a good voice but an unusual style. Rap music was his background as he rapped in the spirit. Once the mood was just right and emotions were running high, he set the stage for his offering.

He criticized preachers for making a long hard pull for money. Then he did the same. He explained the reasons why we should give to him. Remember—it's always about the money. If you need to discover a problem, follow the money trail. The love of money is the root of all evil. Our pastor took from our general fund to match or double what his friend received because the Bible said a prophet was worthy of double honor. We didn't question him; one man was in control of our church. Extortion isn't legal, however some think so, and it happens in churches. The really sad part is, they usually get away with the crime.

Once the money was safely put away, the show began. Their first way to initiate signs and wonders was getting people to fall under the power of God, or the power of suggestion. It didn't matter what made someone fall, as long as it happened. This so-called sign or wonder set the stage for the man's show. The evangelist knew almost every trick and he constantly searched for different ways to deceive. As a last resort, he put his hands on a person and shook as he slowly pushed them to the floor. Why did we think it was the power of God? Our state of mind was—somewhat distorted.

The handy man and family didn't fall. He must have considered the danger because of a back injury he received years before. His wife didn't fall because she knew it was nonsense. Perhaps they didn't know what to think of all the strange things. I wonder what God thought; He sees and knows everything, even what we think. God knows our motives.

Do you suppose their Bible college taught this? I question what is taught in Bible colleges. I'm sure good teachings are prevalent in their school, along with false doctrines. I don't understand why things are taught in churches that aren't in God's Word. Why do educated men teach wrong traditions as if they were Bible? I believe most are deceived.

The evangelist began his show by looking for someone emotional. This was usually a woman or young girl. Emotions can cause one to do things in the flesh, which may appear, in the Spirit. Sometimes women are more emotional than men, but we can be the same way. Once people fell, it set the stage for more nonsense. Enthusiasm and laughter are contagious. Moods and emotions can be altered. Some desire signs, wonders and miracles. They are more susceptible to deception.

It's sad, people are used and brainwashed. They don't realize what is happening. It's deception from the devil, demons, principalities, powers and spiritual wickedness in high places. I pray for the false preachers, for we wrestle not against flesh and blood. (paraphrasing Eph. 6:12)

If God Makes You Fall Great, If Man Makes You Fall Fake

The evangelist made people fall when they were thirty feet away. The trick was accomplished by him shouting something spiritual. He shouted filled, be filled or fire! People were emotional and startled into falling. How do you think it affected the rest of us spiritual, brainwashed people? You guessed it; the freak show continued.

45

People have fallen because of God's power. It's written in the Bible. If God does this for you, it will definitely be good. Some say they had wonderful experiences from falling under the power of God. In my opinion, this is rare. In the rare few instances in the Bible, people didn't fall because they were taught. They didn't fall by someone placing hands on them and praying. Nobody caught people who fell. False prophets use absurd tricks to deceive others. You'll see how ridiculous the exploitation and tricks were. If God makes you fall, great! If man makes you fall, fake! It could be your emotions! Perhaps we got in the flesh...I think so.

As I'm writing this story, I'm overwhelmed with emotion. Just now, I felt guilty because I should have walked a closer walk with God. Nevertheless, "And we know that all things work together for good to them that love God, to them who are the called according to his purpose." (Rom. 8:28) With God's help, things will get better.

Jesus declared, "Beware of false prophets, which come to you in sheep's clothing, but inwardly they are ravening wolves." (Mt.7:15) This means they look like Christians, act and dress like them, but inside they are evil killers. They'll take whatever they can from you. False prophets will destroy your mind, body and assets.

After seeing the fake falls, I began falling. Of course, the evangelist wanted to cast a demon out of me. He thought God let him discern, or gave him a word of knowledge; I had a problem of being too dignified. Since the evangelist had been in the same type of business as me, maybe it takes one to know one. It's very possible someone whispered in his ear. A word of knowledge is sometimes—a word of gossip.

It took two years to realize my pastor and the evangelist fought against me. Being naive, I told the evangelist he could stay in my home the next time he was in town. That was an experience I'll never forget. Maybe it was a good thing; I saw things that needed to be exposed. I didn't expect a pat on the back from the preacher, courtesy would be the standard for most. I'll tell that weird story later.

The handy man enjoyed the revival. His wife and daughters didn't, but tolerated it. Most everyone else enjoyed the show, because a year later, they came back and brought friends. The preacher from Florida held another revival; it made the first one look tame in comparison.

Our preacher was pumped up like the Energizer Bunny. He said every service should have a move of the Holy Ghost. He boldly stated, "If the Holy Ghost isn't moving in a service, I will make Him move. All I have to do is preach His Word, and signs and wonders will follow." Of course, we knew to help signs and wonders come to pass. We were well trained. We definitely wanted more miracles and healings.

He Staggered, With A Slurred Speech And Got Drunk

The second sign or wonder was drunkenness. I'm not talking about alcohol, but drunk in the Spirit. Often, our pastor had us look in the book of Acts. He read where people were drunk in the Spirit, and others thought they had too much wine. He knew where—he was heading. Every time he read these scriptures, he staggered, with a slurred speech and got drunk. I don't know if he was in the Spirit or his flesh. Most of us experienced the same emotion. Have you noticed people follow their leader? I've seen many act the same way as their pastor. Jesus said this would happen. "The disciple is not above his master: but everyone that is perfect shall be as his master." (Luke 6:40) "The disciple is not above his master, nor the servant above his lord. It is enough for the disciple that he be as his master, and the servant as his lord." This is found in Matthew 10:24 and the first part of the next verse. Be careful who you follow; there is a good possibility you'll become like them!

When our pastor's wife began laughing uncontrollably, everyone had a good laugh. Actually, the two signs worked well together; get drunk and then fall, of course in the Spirit. We experienced many false signs, wonders and healings. I'll explain in later chapters.

After the revival, our pastor's sermons were like the style of his friend from Florida. He was angry at times. In a Wednesday night service, his wife stood up and with much anger said, "We did not start this church, so that we could neglect our family. We can't do all of the work in this church. You people are going to have to do more and knock on doors to get more people in this church." I don't believe the tone of her voice inspired anyone, certainly not me.

The pastor admitted he might be causing people to leave. He felt the need to preach a series on love. The series wasn't finished. His sermons weren't delivered in love, and were in vain. A teacher should be familiar with a subject before attempting to teach it. I can't imagine teaching a subject I know nothing about.

The pastor told us to use the restroom facilities before and after the services. The handyman had four daughters and one son. Two of his daughters went to the restroom often. Our pastor became agitated and eventually, it enraged him. One Sunday morning, he exploded on the girls in the middle of his sermon. We have to rebuke at times; it should be constructive. Many don't understand love and struggle with the God kind of love. We should love more like Jesus does. It's important to develop and nurture this.

The handy man finally had enough. He spoke with me concerning a meeting with the pastor. I told him the meeting was a good idea. He knew I tried one on one with our pastor, with no success. The next biblical step is to resolve problems with one or two witnesses.

I spoke to our pastor and set up a meeting that afternoon. After we agreed on a time, our pastor called and moved the meeting up two hours. Just before the meeting, he told us the reason for changing the time; he needed to call a pastor friend, to even the odds or something. Maybe he thought if a fight broke out, he might need someone's help. We hadn't considered such an idea. I thought we could resolve our differences. Apparently, our pastor had something else in mind. It was evident; he didn't like us. The handy man and I were only trying to help.

We met at the church on a Sunday afternoon. Our pastor told us to sit in the pews at the front, with his friend across from us. He looked down and paced nervously back and forth. He asked what our problem was. I stated we had several complaints we needed to discuss. The tone of my voice was exactly like my friend's: quiet and gentle. The pastor replied with a loud, angry voice. "I've been in a lot of meetings like this. I've had pastors rebuke me, scream at me and curse me. I know how ugly these meetings can be. That is why I brought my friend." His friend was a large man and our pastor was ready for a fight. His temper was out of control and disgusting. Pleasant or not, some things have to take place. We didn't cause this bad situation, but dealt with it the best we could.

I asked the handyman to share his complaint first. Of course, he thought the preacher was too harsh with his daughters. Our preacher was defiant, and believed he was in the right. I explained, the girls possibly had a good reason for their restroom visits. I used a soft voice. The preacher exploded and screamed, "You men are not my boss! You can't tell me what to do!" We were shocked at his tone of voice. We spoke softer than before. My next comment was, "Don't you think your rebuke should have been in private?" He adamantly said, "No! I support my decision, and I will not change it." I replied this. "Well, if you won't receive that rebuke, could we move on to the next?" He said, "Yes."

I asked our pastor if he would apologize to the lady who donated the church pews. Often, he trampled her feelings when he said, "I don't like those pews; I want chairs." He was reluctant to accept this advice. His preacher friend replied, "My goodness, I sure wish we had nice pews like this. You should see the old chairs we have to sit on." I tried to further explain how the woman's feelings were hurt. I stated, "God did not give you chairs; He gave you pews; be glad and thankful." I have learned over the years, an apology you have to ask for, usually isn't genuine. I knew that, but I hoped we could help the man.

As he pondered my suggestion, I noticed our pastor do something unusual. He pulled out his cell phone, called the woman and apologized. It was apparent the preacher couldn't deliver a sincere apology. The next complaint was, our pastor was late for services. He was embarrassed in front of his friend. I felt bad for him, so I gently let him off the hook. His friend didn't need to know how many times or how often he was late. I haven't noticed a preacher late for his own services, except him.

Obviously, his college instructors didn't know him well. If they had seen the problems I noticed, surely someone would have recommended a different direction for him. Some are in a profession that really doesn't suit them.

The next concern was mentioned by me. Sometimes near the end of a sermon, our pastor's son became disruptive. One of the qualifications of a pastor is, he rules his own house well. We discussed various methods of dealing with this problem. Our pastor seemed to understand and agreed that he could improve the situation.

The meeting ended with everyone walking in love—we hoped. Hard feelings were developing in our pastor, for my friend and me. His expression showed it. Perhaps the preacher's ego suffered a crushing blow, although unintended. After the meeting, the good man and I took a moment to discuss the situation. I told him I was quitting.

Later, I contacted the woman who started the church. I told her I was leaving. I knew she would call our pastor. He called immediately and was nice. Since I was no longer a member of the church, I rebuked him without being concerned. The rebuke was firm, but done with love. I earnestly tried to help the man. He needed a lot of help and it seemed like I was the only one willing. If someone doesn't confront evil, it will overtake us. It's a tough job, but someone has to.

My pastor apologized; he hoped I wouldn't quit. Twice I asked him to repeat the apology with more sincerity. Finally he convinced me he was sincere. How naive could I be? I forgot how our pastor lied. I shouldn't have gone back, even though I didn't want to frustrate Karen. On second thought, I learned valuable lessons the hard way. Excellent material was obtained that will help others. Hopefully, some will learn from my mistakes and many false teachings can be avoided.

God has many promises for us, if we meet the conditions. Jesus is always praying for us. This causes all things to work together for our good if we love God and are called according to His purpose. I just interpreted Rom. 8:27–28. These two verses should give us comfort.

The good man and I went back to church, as if everything was fine. We hoped and prayed our pastor would change. My friend donated every spare moment to the remodeling. He was sad and sensed his days were numbered at the church, but still wanted to finish his work.

Our pastor asked me to read a letter he was giving the handyman. The letter stated the man should go back to his previous church. The pastor thought he left prematurely. The letter contained legalese and statements which could be used against him. I suggested he tone it down and rewrite it. He laughed and said, "You should have seen the letter before it was revised by someone at my Bible college." His reasoning was, regardless of what the letter said, the man wouldn't be happy. This was probably true, but he could've been nice about it. As usual, my pastor didn't take my advice. I wondered why he even asked me to read the letter. Perhaps, it was a warning to me, if I didn't fully submit.

Sometimes, a letter written in haste can accomplish more than you desire. Letters of this type may display hidden problems, agendas and anger. Many years of hurts can be exposed. We should be careful of things we say, careful of what we put in writing and extremely careful of what we do! I include myself in that rebuke.

At least there was a check for five hundred dollars inside the (you're fired) letter. This would somewhat compensate my friend for his labor donations which ran into thousands of dollars. It was amazing how the timing of the letter coincided with completion of the remodeling. Many people use others to get money and things. We should love people and use money, not love money and use people.

The small check didn't inspire my friend. Maybe it eased the conscience of our pastor. Sometimes a good deed is an attempt to feel better or look good. I'm positive a good deed with a wrong motive is bad. God knows our motives, and He doesn't reward bad behavior. The word punishment comes to my mind.

The next sermon was delivered to one less family. The mood of the pastor was upbeat and gleeful. He was pleased to run off the woman he considered a wolf. Perhaps the pastor viewed me as a wolf. He wouldn't make me leave because he needed Karen. He could influence her to divorce me, without losing her. This may explain why Karen mentioned divorce from time to time. I've heard the stories of preachers causing divorces.

Isn't it astonishing how people cause others to leave churches for no good reason? If a family doesn't impress a religious social club, others remove them from their church. There are biblical reasons for doing this. If someone is doing something horrible and won't listen to reason, the matter should be brought before the church. It should be rare anyone is told to leave. Some harass others until they quit. They don't have valid complaints, so they make them quit, hoping no one notices their evil deeds. Perhaps they say, I don't know why they quit; there was nothing said that should have offended them. It's more than likely most people are run off from churches—for the wrong reasons. It's God's desire we love and forgive others. We don't have to like people; loving them is not an option. We must!

No doubt, our pastor thought he was in the right. He believed people who wouldn't submit were trouble. He viewed them as wolves that couldn't be changed. He explained, "You have to get rid of anyone who is a wolf." I suppose his Bible college taught this as a disciplinary action. Before this story is over, you'll recognize who the wolves were.

CHAPTER SIX

A NEW WOLF ARRIVES

O ur pastor's friend who came to the meeting to referee, invited a few of us to a men's breakfast. We were to meet an evangelist who was supposedly gifted with miracles. There is a gift in the Bible called the working of miracles. I don't know if he had the gift, but he was in the ministry a long time, over twenty years. He was experienced and seemed well educated.

His eyes darted quickly from one person to another. Perhaps the man was using his gift of discernment to determine what he could get away with. I'm looking into the past. People say; hindsight is 20/20. I didn't know then, what I know now. I was looking for good in him; eventually, I saw the bad.

It took a long time to determine this man was a false prophet. Sometimes, it's like putting a puzzle together, without realizing what it will look like when completed. This can take a very long time.

The older preacher got everyone excited about increasing our church membership. He said, "What really brings people in, is when they hear about the miracles." The man was selling himself; our pastor bought it.

He asked the evangelist to preach; he was hoping for signs, wonders and of course, miracles. He thought God would use the evangelist to increase our attendance. The young pastor didn't get what he desired and our church dwindled.

In our next service our pastor was excited, even though he had bad news. He said it like this, "I must confess, I got a speeding ticket on the way to church today, glory to God!" The glory to God comment was stated with—too much emphasis. The glory to God remark was used often after a sentence. Sometimes a good saying is expressed at the wrong time and sounds ridiculous.

Several people in our church had the habit of saying this, even if their comment was negative. I don't understand how something bad could bring glory to God. One day I asked the main spiritual lady in our church, "Why do you almost always end a sentence with the words, glory to God?" She read a scripture in the Bible where we are always to give glory to God. I asked her, "If you were involved in a tragic accident, and one of your family members was ripped apart, would you tell the story and end it with glory to God?" She said, "Yes, I would." I wasn't sarcastic with the lady; I just wanted to know why they said this.

Some people over use the phrase, praise God. They use it too often at the beginning or end of a sentence. When a negative statement is completed with either phrase, it's almost like they mock God. Sometimes we act too spiritual and don't realize what we're saying.

I use sensationalism to shock or startle people into reality. Some are deep in denial of their personal faults and can't be helped. They need to help themselves and repent. If we have serious faults, early repentance can help avoid a premature death.

Before I get into the new wolf story, I must give more background on our pastor. Perhaps you'll understand, I had high hopes of the older man being a role model for him. The younger evangelist wasn't a good influence on our pastor; neither was the older. You'll see, the story gets more bizarre as it continues. Perhaps I was a part of the nonsense—so I could expose it.

One day, our pastor told us about a toy his son wanted. The father looked everywhere, but couldn't find it. He agreed in prayer with his son that someone would make the toy. When our pastor told this story, he seemed confident, someone would have to manufacture it. He believed he could pray and have whatever he wanted. Why didn't he demand ten million dollars and retire? Intelligent people who have college degrees should know—we can't always have what we want. At times everyone needs a reality check. Positive thinking is good if it lines up with His Holy Word.

We Have To Pray According To God's Will

I tried many times in the past to advise my pastor; he resented it. He could quote these scriptures. "And this is the confidence that we have in Him, that, if we ask anything according to His will, He heareth us: And if we know that He hears us, whatsoever we ask, we know that we have the petitions that we desired of Him." (1 John 5:14–15) Often our will is wrong and God's is always right. I'm glad He answers our prayers according to His will.

Somehow, he didn't grasp the fact, we have to pray according to God's will. The man thought he could ask for anything in the name of Jesus and get it. God promised He would supply our needs, not necessarily our wants. He rewards us if we seek to please Him. We should seek God first, His kingdom and righteousness; then the things we need will be provided. I'm interpreting Matthew 6:31–33.

Karen and I often had discussions about our pastor. She got angry when I spoke against him. I asked her if she could pray and ask for a new toy for me. I wanted a one hundred foot long submarine to float up in my front yard, without any water floating it. I wanted it to weigh about three tons and be manned by a crew of twenty men. I wanted it painted purple with pink polka dots. I asked Karen to demand that God deliver it right now. She became more angry. Sometimes we might shock or startle a person into reality. Perhaps my sensationalism went too far and turned into sarcasm. *Lord, please forgive me, in Jesus name.*

The weather forecast was indicating an ice storm one cold winter day. I told our pastor he might need to cancel the next service. He said, "Oh no—I will pray and it will only be a cold rain." The pastor had to cancel because of the ice. I asked him what happened to his prayer to change the storm. He said, "You have to start early with something like that, in order for it to work."

His lies began to bother me. At first, I tried to give our pastor the benefit of the doubt. I told myself, it was inadvertent or he just misspoke. It couldn't be a lie, certainly not! Surely he knew what the Bible says about liars. They don't go to heaven when they die. John says in Revelation "...But the fearful, and unbelieving, and the abominable, and murderers, and whoremongers, and sorcerers, and idolaters, and all liars shall have their part in the lake which burneth with fire and brimstone: which is the second death." (Rev. 21:8)

One day, my pastor called and asked if I knew a certain man. I told him, I knew the man. He asked if the man drank alcohol and used drugs. I told him, if I didn't see the man doing these things and said he did, I would be gossiping. He declared, "Yes, you are correct." Then I stated, "If you said the man did these things, without seeing him do them, then you would be gossiping." He declared, "No, I wasn't talking about him. I was talking about someone else." The man just told me a bold-faced lie!

I told our pastor that I spoke to the landlord who owned the church building. I explained, he was upset because our rent was late. The preacher shouted, "He is a liar! I've never been late except maybe one time!" Later, the owner verified our pastor was late numerous times. I believed the owner of the building; he was my friend. I negotiated the lease agreement at the beginning with the landlord. We had a good agreement and the rent was discounted four hundred and fifty dollars per month. The owner also donated one hundred dollars per month to our church. Our pastor didn't show gratitude. I assume anyone would conclude our pastor was confused, and struggled with expressing love.

Our visiting evangelist was a marvel to behold. He was pleased we were taught how to receive from God. (fall down) I didn't see any verifiable miracles, but I believe some were healed.

One lady declared she was healed of fibromyalgia. She said this, even many years later. It's possible she received her healing like the woman in the Bible with the issue of blood. The woman knew she would be healed, if she only touched the hem of Jesus' garment. Jesus explained; her faith made her whole. Faith is the key to many blessings. Some understand the power in the name of Jesus Christ.

God's Word Is His Will

The reason many don't receive healing today, they don't understand how simple it is. They believe it may not be God's desire to heal them. God's Word is His will. His Word contains scriptures which say, it is His will to heal. If you pray, and ask God to heal you if it be His will, there is no faith in that prayer. The word if contains doubt and unbelief. Praying if it be your will, is proper for certain things. Look at this. "Go to now, ye that say, To day or to morrow we will go into such a city, and continue there a year, and buy and sell, and get gain: Whereas ye know not what shall be on the morrow. For what is your life? It is even a vapour, that appeareth for a little time, and then vanisheth away. For that ye ought to say, if the Lord will, we shall live, and do this, or that." (James 4:13–15) Sometimes we aren't healed in this life and can't understand why; we will surely be healed in heaven.

We must pray according to God's will to get results. If you call for the elders of the church to anoint with oil and pray, this is appropriate. You would be following the Bible. This method is much better than one on one, where someone could get prideful at their special anointing.

I asked my pastor to pray for an adjustment on my lower back. We prayed this before. This time it was different. Slowly I lifted my legs while sitting in the pew. God made the adjustment before my pastor had a chance to pray. He became more excited than me. I wasn't surprised.

It felt good as my shorter left leg became longer than my right, then shortened to the same length. It reminded me of years before when a chiropractor measured my legs. He worked until the shorter leg was the same as the other. Glory to God and not the false prophet. God has healed me many times, in fact every time. Some day this body may not heal, but God gives us a glorified body that lasts forever.

Good things happened at the full gospel church. If the pastor had taken advice from his elders, perhaps he would have surrendered to God, walked in love, and wouldn't have been deceived. People mean well, but try too hard and miss the glory God shares and reveals in us.

Look in 2 Cor. 3:18. "But we all, with open face beholding as in a glass the glory of the Lord, are changed into the same image from glory to glory, even as by the Spirit of the Lord." The Bible declares this. "For I reckon that the sufferings of this present time are not worthy to be compared with the glory which shall be revealed in us." (Rom. 8:18) The more humble we are, the more we'll see God's glory. We shouldn't seek glory, instead we should glory in the cross and what Jesus did for us.

Pride can develop before we realize it and we can regard ourselves too highly. Some forget 2 Cor. 4:7. "But we have this treasure in earthen vessels, that the excellency of the power may be of God, and not of us." (Phil. 2:3) "Let nothing be done through strife or vainglory; but in lowliness of mind let each esteem others better than themselves." Consider others, greater or better than you.

Pride goes before destruction. The Bible makes this clear; everything must be done with love. A person could be very good and nothing like a false prophet, but still end up in the same place with them. Evil people and demonic spirits would be no fun to be with. My point is—it takes more than being a good person.

Accept Jesus Christ as your Savior; walk the walk, and live a surrendered life so you can call Him—Lord. Learn about His Word and be transformed by the renewing of your mind. When something is broken, take a look at the owner's manual. We desperately need His Word! It's the guide to show us the way. "How sweet are thy words unto my taste! yea, sweeter than honey to my mouth! Through thy precepts I get understanding: therefore I hate every false way. Thy word is a lamp unto my feet and a light unto my path." (Ps. 119:103–105)

His Word can heal, if you let it build up your faith. He will supply all your needs, bless you beyond measure, and give you peace which passes all understanding. His Word will help you grow into the measure of the stature and fullness of Christ.

We can own what God owns. Would you give up what you have for what God has? Wow, what a deal! If you desire to be like Him, it's yours for the asking. All we have to give up is our selfishness. All we truly own is our bad habits. God owns everything.

The old evangelist, had some tricks up his sleeve. (figuratively speaking) Sometimes, he moved his arms over someone's head as he prayed for the bands to be severed which had them bound. He liked to cast demons out of people whether they had any or not. Men like him want to feel and act super spiritual. They want the power of God to work through them. God's power would work, if they wouldn't try so hard. Exalting one's self is not biblical or spiritual; being humble is. God doesn't need our help and we need to get out of His way. Often, we prevent His help, by doing things our way.

Billy Graham is a good example of someone who is very humble. Because of this, people have exalted him. Because of his humility, the best miracle of all—salvation has come to thousands, if not millions. Even false prophets say salvation is the greatest miracle. They should focus on it and stop doing tricks, false things, and fake falls. Why do we do things in church that aren't in the Bible? Some won't do what is written. It makes me question what inspires or motivates them. Maybe they serve a false god; it's very possible. God declared, "Thou shalt have no other gods before me." (Ex. 20:3)

The older evangelist made people fall by blowing his breath on them. He laid hands on them and prayed. He wanted rid of a demon one Sunday afternoon. The service was over and only a few were left: Karen, me, the pastor, his wife and the evangelist. The older man said, "Brother, we need to pray for you." I asked him, "What for?" He said, "Your wife said you had a spirit of perfection in you." I quickly replied, "No way sir, she cast that thing out of me years ago!" We all had a good laugh. Many episodes at our church were laughable; some weren't. At times they were more than disgusting.

It Was No Laughing Matter

The older man tried to cast a demon out of a beautiful young lady. It was no laughing matter. There were a lot of people at church. The way the woman moved around on the floor, as if she were in pain, was an awful sight. The evangelist screamed at her for a long time. He couldn't get rid of the evil spirit. The man's show was ugly and disrespectful.

No demons were revealed but other things were as she rolled on the floor. I felt sorry for her and I'm sure her daughter did. Our pastor finally dismissed the service. He selected a few people to continue the show in a back room. To my knowledge, no one knew what happened. Confusion is caused by the devil and evil spirits; they work through people. If you can imagine things getting worse; they did.

The next day in Healing School, the evangelist told a few of us what type of demon he was dealing with. He said this type was one of the most difficult to cast out. If what the preacher said was true, he shouldn't reveal it to others. Some things are private, and should be kept that way.

I desired to inform the lady what the preacher said about her. I wanted to know if he was telling the truth. I knew if Karen found out I told her, she would probably divorce me. These false prophets were a source of contention in our marriage. She threatened divorce before.

She Looked Shocked

A week or two after Karen died, I visited the woman. After a nice talk with the lady, her husband and daughter, I asked her husband if I could have a private conversation with his wife. The lady's husband and daughter left. My patience paid off; I discovered what I suspected.

When I mentioned the evil spirit the preacher said she had, she looked shocked. The lady was calm as she explained she didn't have the problems the older evangelist declared. She confessed some faults in her past. It wasn't necessary for her to confess to me. I believe she did to prove she was being honest. The lady was humble and convincing as she conversed with me. I felt sure, the preacher lied about her like he did on other matters. Suddenly she knew why people acted different to her.

Her husband knew something was wrong with our church. He found another one they were happy with. They needed to leave; in fact, all of us needed to move on. I suppose some feel trapped in a horrible church. In the past, some statements the older man made were lies. Now, everything adds up to—false prophet.

I asked the older evangelist to let me ride in his fast car one Sunday afternoon. This was before I knew he was a false prophet. He claimed his car had five hundred horsepower. When I was young, I had a car with four hundred. I was curious about the additional power. The man explained, he asked God if he could have the car. He said God told him he could have it, if he promised he wouldn't kill anyone. That sounded logical to me, so I climbed in and we took off. As we entered a straight stretch of highway, I asked him to get on it. When he stepped on the accelerator, I screamed at the preacher to stop. He scared me so bad, I thought he would kill someone.

What I hoped and prayed for wasn't happening. My pastor wasn't influenced in a positive way. He became more bizarre and strange. I realize Christians should be peculiar, but we should know right from wrong. We'll be judged; some preachers will be at the judgment for lost people. "For we must all appear before the judgment seat of Christ; that everyone may receive the things done in his body, according to that he hath done, whether it be good or bad." (2 Cor. 5:10)

My pastor told ushers to avoid getting too drunk in the Spirit. He stated, "You can control how drunk you get in the Spirit, and should control it, so you'll be alert enough to perform your duties." He said, "I have to control myself like that or I wouldn't be able to preach." I'm glad he could control himself and not get too drunk; he should have used control in other areas as well!

It Is Like Monkey See, Monkey Do

He instructed, "If you want to know how to act in a service, watch me. It is like monkey see, monkey do. Just do like I do. I am your leader and you should follow your leader." I wondered what he meant about controlling—drunk in the Spirit. If we could control it, then maybe we were creating it. A few years later, I was sure it was created. I tried to overlook things in our church, so Karen wouldn't get upset.

Karen read her Bible and prayed more than me; she was probably right and I was wrong. Spouses should submit to each other. Look in Ephesians 5:21. "Submitting yourselves one to another in the fear of God." The proper roles of a husband and wife are explained.

Our pastor collected information on supernatural things, especially from his two mentors, the older and younger evangelists. One story came from the man who founded the college they attended. The elderly preacher was speaking to his students, when he abruptly froze, as if he were paralyzed. The man was motionless for several minutes before he resumed speaking, as if nothing happened. It may have been emotions.

Our pastor said the way signs and wonders worked in his life was like this: "I see myself in my mind doing something, and then later, I just do it." He believed God had shown him, in advance, how He would do a sign or wonder through him. I thought it could be—in his mind. It's called in the flesh or emotions, and it occurs naturally.

We Should Be Careful Which Thoughts We Act On

I'm sure when God does a sign or wonder, He does it without us thinking about it ahead of time. He does the signs and wonders; we don't. God gives us good and helpful thoughts. It's demons (invisible spirit beings) who put ugly thoughts in our minds, hoping we'll act on them. This is how the devil works; he can't be everywhere like God, so he instructs evil spirits to put thoughts in our minds. We should be careful which thoughts we act on. I'm sure, I shouldn't be so quick to speak or act on a thought in my mind. Perhaps, I should run it through a filter—the Holy Bible.

God's Word is the most powerful thing we could have, if it's in our heart. We must be a doer of the Word. "But be ye doers of the word, and not hearers only, deceiving your own selves." (James 1:22) Hide His Word in your heart and do it. We can't make it to heaven, without doing His Word.

The Bible says, "...for out of the abundance of the heart, the mouth speaketh." (Mt.12:34) "...for as he thinketh in his heart so is he" (Prov. 23:7) We should think on things that are true, honest, just, pure, lovely, virtue and praise. If we meditate on these thoughts, and they fill our heart to abundance, we'll speak and do what we should. This is a simple formula—think right, and speak right, so we can do right. Please don't forget, "Death and life are in the power of the tongue." (Prov. 18:21) *Father, please help us think, speak and do your word, amen.*

After our pastor told of the preacher becoming paralyzed, he did the same thing. He read in the Old Testament, where someone's tongue cleaved to the roof of his mouth. Then our pastor stood motionless, with his mouth open, and one arm in the air. He was in this state for a few minutes; before he began speaking as if nothing happened.

Later, I was sitting on the front pew. My mind convinced me that my body from the waist down couldn't move. When our mind does that, we can't move! That is how our body works; the brain sends signals. I mentioned this to the pastor. He smiled with approval and thought it was a sign from God. Remember him saying, monkey see and monkey do? Could we say, the power of suggestion? Perhaps it was our emotions or flesh. Some call it witchcraft, control and brain-washing. I was acting like my pastor, shame on me. Can you see what happens when we follow someone who isn't where they should be spiritually?

The mind is delicate; it can be manipulated and altered. We can renew our mind with God's Word. That is exactly what I'm doing, trying to restore my mind. I'm allowing myself to become as potter's clay and let the Creator shape and mold me into what He knows is best. A friend of mine didn't do something that I requested. I said without thinking, "I will make you do it." The quick reply was, "You can't make me do anything!" I said, "Oh, you're right." Without realizing it, I was hurting my friend with the same hurt I was hurt with—control. I asked my friend and God to forgive me. I didn't think before I spoke. I don't want to hurt anyone or my Heavenly Father. He knows everything.

There is only one solution to this problem. We must become filled with the Holy Spirit, so we can walk in the light as He is in the light. He will cleanse us from all unrighteousness. It's walking in the truth; Jesus is the truth and light! "But if we walk in the light, as He is in the light, we have fellowship one with another, and the blood of Jesus Christ His Son cleanseth us from all sin. If we say that we have no sin, we deceive ourselves, and the truth is not in us. If we confess our sins, He is faithful and just to forgive us our sins, and to cleanse us from all unrighteousness. If we say that we have not sinned, we make Him a liar, and His word is not in us." (1 John 1:7–10)

1 John 2:27 states, "But the anointing which ye have received of Him abideth in you, and ye need not that any man teach you: but as the same anointing teacheth you of all things, and is truth, and is no lie, and even as it hath taught you, ye shall abide in Him." We remain in Him, if we allow God's Spirit to teach us. Jesus explained this to His disciples. "If ye keep my commandments, ye shall abide in my love; even as I have kept my Father's commandments, and abide in his love." (John 15:10)

(John 15:12–14) "This is my commandment, That ye love one another, as I have loved you. Greater love hath no man than this, that a man lay down his life for his friends. Ye are my friends, if ye do whatsoever I command you." Jesus gave His all so we can have everything He is heir to. He expects us to give our all. Think about it—doesn't this seem like a fair trade?

No one knows the persecution or trials we may encounter. Many Christians have died because of their faith in Jesus Christ. Would our faith be strong enough?

We Ought To Lay Down Our Lives For The Brethren

1 John 3:16 says, "Hereby perceive we the love of God, because He laid down His life for us: and we ought to lay down our lives for the brethren." Most likely, we won't have to die saving someone's life. We should be willing to, if necessary.

Romans 13:14 states clearly, "But put ye on the Lord Jesus Christ, and make not provision for the flesh, to fulfill the lusts thereof." Take a look at Romans 12:1. "I beseech you therefore brethren, by the mercies of God, that ye present your bodies a living sacrifice, holy, acceptable unto God, which is your reasonable service." It's God's will that we live.

For many years, I was disappointed with religion. I tried an easier way. I realized the way I chose, was difficult. As I slowly backslid, I forgot sin causes death. My eating habits, along with other sins, were slowly destroying me. Sometimes we can't see these problems until we experience a tragedy.

After the sudden death of Karen, I realized I wanted to live and not only to have life, but life more abundantly. I chose to take the advice of Jesus. His way is easier than ours and not impossible as some would think. We suffer whether we're saved or not. I would rather suffer with God's help than without it.

Jesus said in Mt. 11:30, "For my yoke is easy, and my burden is light." If we walk in the natural or flesh, we always get things backwards. If we walk in the Spirit, we will with our Father's help, have victory. When Jesus made that statement over 2000 years ago, He knew people understood what a yoke was for. They used them to fasten oxen together to pull heavy loads. He wants to help with the burdens of life. Jesus Christ can help lighten our load and make life easier.

"For whatsoever is born of God overcometh the world: and this is the victory that overcometh the world, even our faith." (1 John 5:4) "Delight thyself also in the Lord; and He shall give thee the desires of thine heart." (Psalm 37:4) I've experienced this blessing many times in my life. The better we live, the more God rewards us. Look at this. "...and I will recompense them according to their deeds, and according to the works of their own hands." That was the last part of Jer. 25:14. "For we must all appear before the judgment seat of Christ; that everyone may receive the things done in his body, according to that he hath done, whether it be good or bad." (2 Cor. 5:10)

Everywhere the Bible states we can have what we ask for, there are conditions we must meet, before these prayers will work. Pray according to God's will, so He will answer your prayers. We should live a life of complete surrender to God. Don't have other gods before Him. Keep His commandments. Remember, love covers a multitude of sins. If you love people and God, it will show. You can have His favor, protection and enjoy a long life. This seems hard at first, but in reality our life is more difficult if we don't follow Jesus. "Confess your faults one to another, and pray one for another, that ye may be healed. The effectual fervent prayer of a righteous man availeth much." (James 5:16)

Anyone can lose everything. Job was a wealthy man and lost it all, including his health. Job confessed—the thing he feared the most came on him. If you're in serious trouble, do like Job. As he prayed for his friends, his life turned around. "And the Lord turned the captivity of Job, when he prayed for his friends: also the Lord gave Job twice as much as he had before." (Job 42:10) This is how I pray: *Lord, thank you for this wonderful day. Thank you for all of your blessings. Praise your Holy name. Lord, forgive me of my sins; help me to walk in the light as you are in the light.*

Take a close look at John 8:12. "Then spake Jesus again unto them, saying, I am the light of the world: he that followeth me shall not walk in darkness, but shall have the light of life." John 9:5 declares, "As long as I am in the world, I am the light of the world." John 1:4 says, "In Him was life; and the life was the light of men." Do you remember the old expression; I saw the light? When we see His light, we'll see clearly.

I ask God to guide me. He is a lamp unto my feet and a light unto my path. Then I ask Him to bless my friends, family, and enemies. I pray this prayer differently each day so it won't be vain repetition. Sometimes we converse with Him in meditation, in short sentences or thoughts. "Praying always with all prayer and supplication in the Spirit..." (Eph. 6:18) This is the first part of the verse. We must acknowledge God in all our ways.

We talk with God when we pray, and we hear from Him when we read His Word. The Bible says to meditate on His Word day and night. If you feel like you're not praying enough, I know how you feel. There is nothing wrong with listening—more than we speak. In our meditation and thoughts we're speaking more than we realize. Some people might pray enough but fail to listen through meditating or studying His Word. This could be why we fail to have abundant life. Some pray and read His Word enough, but fail to do it.

There is good in everyone, even false prophets. A false prophet said, "If you want the Word to work, you will have to work the Word." It is easier said than done, but essential. He is the solution to all problems. His Word is our roadmap or owner's manual and the way to eternal life in heaven.

CHAPTER SEVEN

THE YOUNG WOLF COMES BACK

It was almost a year since we saw the wild and radical preacher, the younger evangelist. My pastor informed me, the preacher was accepting my offer to stay in our home. My pastor and his evangelist friend, decided to have a week-long revival. The evangelist was bringing a friend who would be in charge of praise and worship.

Our pastor asked me to pick up the two gentlemen at the airport. He informed me, I would need a van to transport their luggage and a large keyboard. The evangelist's friend was great on the piano. At the airport the preacher shoved his luggage toward me. I didn't appreciate being treated as his servant. Of course, I didn't let him know he offended me.

On the way home, we discussed what they liked to eat. I informed them I would purchase these items while they relaxed in my home. One would think the preacher would be nice with all the free services. I discovered the evangelist didn't want to be friends with me. He said if we were buddies or pals, I wouldn't receive his sermons as well. He wanted to control people and be on a higher level. Humility wasn't one of his attributes. Arrogance is so unacceptable in anyone. I enjoyed being friends with preachers and wished I could be friends with our pastor. However, he said the same thing about friendships.

They Wanted To See Signs And Wonders

The two men expected nice things from us, but they didn't believe it was required of them. The Bible informs; be good to other Christians. "As we have therefore opportunity, let us do good unto all men, especially unto them who are of the household of faith." (Gal. 6:10)

The preachers desired to pray for us as long as we fell to the floor, laughed, danced, or ran. They wanted signs, wonders and miracles at their command. They wanted everyone to honor and respect them in a special way. People were supposed to esteem them greater and be their servants. The evangelist said we should treat them better than a king. Jesus said, "But he that is greatest among you shall be your servant." (Mt. 23:11) A good preacher will serve—without being served.

The piano man was nice and I respected him. He seemed content with the food Karen and I provided. He sang music that he wrote. Karen purchased a CD of his, I will always cherish. I believe he will play his piano and sing in heaven. The man loved everyone and didn't demand things of me. The preacher was the opposite and before the week was over, I was angry. I forgave him every time, and he didn't know I was offended. I've always tried to give someone the benefit of the doubt.

During that week, I didn't schedule much work. Karen and I desired to serve our guests and be rested for the services. The evangelist insulted me with this comment. "Tony, you must be doing something wrong, to not have any more business than you have." Since he had a carpet cleaning business before, he told me how to operate my business. I didn't like his advice; his bragging always got in the way.

The intensity of the revival grew as the week progressed. The number of people also increased each night. By the end of the week, we had about eighty people. The man had a very impressive show. That was precisely what it was—a show. I didn't know this at the time.

God wasn't a part of the nonsense. God doesn't promote evil or sin. It's created by our actions! God's permissive will isn't a good saying. Some things He permits are not His will; He doesn't want anyone spending eternity in hell. The Lord is not willing that anyone perish, but that all should repent. He permits it by allowing free will.

A woman drove a long distance to our church. She learned of our meetings on the internet. Perhaps she searched the words: signs, wonders and miracles. She seemed nice. However, there was something strange about her. She explained, that she was a God chaser. She was hungry for more of God; well so was I.

Many Christians desire a closer walk with God. Some hunger and thirst after righteousness, and some signs and wonders. This woman was seeking the supernatural. When we realized how much the evangelist liked her, we assumed she was okay. We were in for a shock.

I met the lady during her first visit. She was following the young man, seeking miracles. Less than two minutes into our conversation, she told of bizarre things in other churches. She revealed her gift of praying.

The lady prayed for people's fillings in their teeth to become gold. When she noticed I had this desire she said, "Your fillings are gold; go look in the mirror." I hesitated. She insisted, "Go to the bathroom and look in the mirror." As I walked to the restroom, I hoped God had miraculously changed my silver fillings to gold. My excitement increased as I thought how wonderful this would be.

When I looked in the mirror, I saw a gold filling in one tooth. As I saw this, I thought—no way. After I had that thought, the gold changed to silver. I assumed my mind was playing tricks on me, and maybe the lady was crazy. Then I thought, maybe I'm not spiritual enough.

When I described this story to the spiritual ladies, they thought the woman was weird. We told our pastor, so he would know we might have trouble in our services. I presume the young evangelist was informed.

The next time the evangelist saw the woman in our church, he said, "God has shown you unusual things. Don't give holy things to dogs; and don't cast your pearls before the swine." The scripture for this is found in Mt. 7:6. "Give not that which is holy unto the dogs, neither cast ye your pearls before swine, lest they trample them under their feet, and turn again and rend you." The man was glad she was spiritual. He was warning her about people who weren't. In essence, he called us dogs and pigs. Would God give someone a word of knowledge, knowing they would misuse it? Perhaps our pastor informed him of the unusual lady.

Of course, we believed the woman after his rebuke, and wanted to be spiritual like her. After several encounters, she finally convinced me I had gold fillings. I was ready to get in my car when the woman said, "Tony, do you mind if I pray for you?" I asked what for? She said, "For you to get gold fillings." I agreed with her in the name of Jesus for my miracle; suddenly there was a taste in my mouth like metal.

When we arrived at home, I went to a mirror and saw gold fillings. Karen looked and saw the same. The next service, I showed my gold teeth to everyone. A strange thing happened; most everyone saw my fillings as gold, but some didn't. They saw a dark silver color. I realize our minds can be changed, and brainwashed. Our minds were playing tricks. One tooth had a gold cross that glowed!

Sometimes, we see things that don't exist. I'm sure about one thing; writing this story is prompting me to study the Bible. Studying the Word of God will renew a person's mind.

Strange things can bother us. Apostle Paul was bothered with a thorn in the flesh. The Bible said, it was the messenger of Satan sent to buffet him, so he would not be exalted above measure. A messenger of Satan is not a sickness or disease. It's an evil spirit. Three times Paul asked God to remove it. God told Paul, His grace was sufficient for him. I believe God was telling Paul; with My help, you can overcome the evil spirit.

Someday, God will remove the devil and evil spirits. That time has not come. Through adversity and problems, we'll learn to overcome. We are more than conquerors through Jesus. "...greater is He that is in you, than he that is in the world." (1 John 4:4) Read about Paul's thorn in the flesh in 2 Cor. 12:4–10.

The false prophets were using an evil spirit to extort money; it was the spirit of fear. You can find it in 2 Tim. 1:7. "For God hath not given us the spirit of fear; but of power, and of love, and of a sound mind." Some words have opposite meanings. Fear can be sin or a reverence for God. Fear of

God is good and helps us stay on the straight and narrow path. A spirit of fear is bad. Since God hasn't given this, it's obviously an evil spirit. Let's call it what it is—a demon!

The preachers used Old Testament scriptures to scare us. (Mal. 3:8–9) "Will a man rob God? Yet ye have robbed Me. But ye say, Wherein have we robbed thee? In tithes and offerings. Ye are cursed with a curse: for ye have robbed Me, even this whole nation." We should study the New Testament on giving. I'm not implying we shouldn't tithe. We shouldn't use God's Word to extort money. God wants us to give out of love, not compulsion. Some preachers accuse us of robbing God, but they want to steal from us.

The next few verses after Malachi 3:9 tell the tremendous benefits of tithing; it's good to give. Some of the Old Testament was fulfilled and replaced by God's new covenant. Please look at this verse. "Christ hath redeemed us from the curse of the law, being made a curse for us: for it is written, cursed is everyone that hangeth on a tree:" (Gal. 3:13)

The New Testament explains how to give in 2 Cor. 9:7. "Every man according as he purposeth in his heart, so let him give; not grudgingly or of necessity: for God loveth a cheerful giver." If we're taught a curse would come on us if we didn't tithe, we would give out of necessity, for fear of punishment. How could we give cheerfully, or as we purpose in our heart? We were taught, blessings only come from offerings, which go above your tithe. The fact is, God blesses everyone, even those who don't tithe. We can't buy blessings; our giving should be as we purpose.

The young evangelist inspired our pastor to ignore some of the New Testament. Occasionally, the men taught 2 Cor. 9:7. They accelerated through this scripture with lightning speed. They tried to convince us how we should purpose in our heart. This tithing sermon lasted about twenty minutes, in almost every service. They called it the tithing sermon. This, and other unbiblical practices, were causing people to leave. The church didn't decrease in attendance for almost another year. Most visitors didn't return. Perhaps they considered most of our services repulsive and absurd. I couldn't see it then; but I see it now.

There was a lack of love from our pastor and his wife. It's possible people noticed pride and arrogance. The pastor, esteeming himself greater than us, was a problem. Some say, I love you, while attempting to control. When threats are made, it's a sign of control. The expression, I sure love you—becomes empty words. I prefer to see it than hear it.

Sometimes our pastor said, "Wow, my hands are on fire! Does anyone need healing?" Trying to convey honor, glory and attention to one's self isn't biblical. He told lies, and that doesn't impress anyone, neither do fake signs and wonders. In the end, they become disgusting.

The church slowly died a disgraceful death. I tried to help the young man avoid this. Twelve months before the church shut down, I quit. I chose to leave before I was fired. The pastor bragged about starting the church. He said no one could fire him, and he wouldn't quit. After about three and a half years, many people fired him. With a few women as his only support, he quit. Karen was devastated.

The young evangelist confessed a lust problem in his past. He told me he didn't want to be alone with my wife, while he was a guest in our home. I didn't want him alone with my wife for one second. Karen agreed with me. He was a preacher; but, I didn't trust him. Eventually you'll discover someone's true character!

It was mostly women who fell and were caught by ushers. I wasn't the head usher, but I took the job serious. The ladies trusted me; they knew I wouldn't let them get hurt. It's dangerous to fall and shouldn't be encouraged. As the women fell into my arms, I carefully laid them on the floor. It seems more disgusting now than it did then. I didn't know then what I know now. Sometimes, I had a thought I shouldn't have. I quickly dismissed it and continued with my duties. The way some of the women smiled, it's possible they had impure thoughts as well. I didn't see anything good come from it.

I became deeply saddened and ashamed, I was a part of that church. At least I held back the tears this time. I asked my Heavenly Father to forgive me. To write this story, I have to look back. Someday, I hope to never look back; my healing will be complete. The Lord knows; I need all kinds of healing.

James 5:16 tells us, "Confess your faults one to another, and pray one for another, that ye may be healed. The effectual fervent prayer of a righteous man availeth much." Some believe God's kingdom is divided against itself. Jesus taught; every kingdom divided against itself—shall not stand. If someone doesn't receive healing, they should search the scriptures. Most likely it's our fault. Some like to blame God. Healing is God's will. Study His Word and have faith. Faith can move mountains. I'm paraphrasing Mt. 17:20.

In God's Word, people rarely fell because of His power. No one fell because someone laid hands on them and prayed. No elders or deacons caught others as they fell. It's a wrong tradition. If someone wants to fall, they could take turns praying and falling in their home. That way things done in churches can be decent and in order.

Everyone should look at the last thing Jesus said before he left this earth in Mark 16:14–18. This is called The Great Commission. Jesus was teaching his disciples. Look at the last part of the last verse. "...they shall lay hands on the sick, and they shall recover."

Jesus was referring to believers or saved people. He didn't say it like this. They shall lay hands on the sick, and they shall fall under my power. Ushers shall catch and lay them down gently so no one will be in a lawsuit; then they shall recover. Before you finish this story, you'll realize why this practice should stop. It is emotionalism, walking in the flesh, and it's dangerous.

Why don't we try a test, to see if this is God or flesh? Place a large sign in front of the church; ushers will no longer catch someone if they fall. If you want God to make you fall, ask Him to catch you! People would understand—how wrong they were when no one fell. Intelligent preachers can provide safety and security for people, without creating an incentive for emotionalism. What would be wrong with asking people to sit for prayer instead of standing? It makes perfect sense.

The young evangelist got excited as the attendance increased each night of the revival. His services were long. He claimed if people stayed for the entire service, they would see God's anointing get stronger. I suppose the preacher meant signs, wonders, and miracles would be more prevalent and spectacular. Well, I was there and it didn't happen, even though I watched closely.

The evangelist told stories of people in other churches that saw unusual and bizarre things. He said in one service rain fell inside the building, only in the first and second pews. We had pews in our church. Perhaps this story was designed to make us stay the two or three hours he would be there. I stayed because I had ushering duties. If God was doing something supernatural, I wanted to see it.

Another church had feathers lying around after the meeting. He claimed these were left by angels. Other meetings had gold dust scattered around. People struggle with vain imaginations. "Why do the heathen rage and the people imagine a vain thing?" (Ps. 2:1) God knows we are weak. Don't use this to justify sin; we can't validate sin.

We didn't have rain or angel feathers in our building. People saw gold specks; it looked like glitter. Some said it would appear on people and soon vanish. Others experienced oil on their heads and hands. It disappeared quickly. This happened to me. Looking back, I believe it was perspiration rather than supernatural. I'm positive the two preachers mentioned the oil before anyone noticed it.

I believe the power of suggestion, along with the fact we longed for God's power, created this. Sometimes the oil experience is genuine, and from God; at times it's emotionalism. People can be brainwashed; it happened to us and can happen to anyone.

When the revival was near the end, the evangelist laid hands on people so quickly, we found it impossible to catch everyone. It was obvious he didn't care if someone fell on the concrete. There were no accidents except for one woman. She was elderly and almost blind. The woman claimed her back was broken. Her claims were loud and clear. It was a scary moment and uncalled for!

The man almost panicked as he told people to pray in the Spirit. She seemed alright, but his prayers for her blindness didn't work. The bigger miracles didn't happen. The signs, wonders and healings we saw could have been imagined or faked. If my prayers don't work, I'll call for elders of the church, and have them anoint me with oil and pray. That way, I'll be doing what the Bible says. If we followed the Bible, God would give us miracles—without a freak show.

The evangelist taught our pastor how to make the supernatural flow. When a person came up for prayer, one foot couldn't be in front of the other. Perhaps that was too much balance and stability. The people were instructed to place their feet together and shoulder width apart. They were told to close their eyes and raise their hands. As the preacher prayed, they were informed there it is, there it is, receive it, receive it! Of course, the preacher could say filled, filled, very loud or fire, fire. A gentle push from the preacher worked, when he laid hands on them. The older evangelist liked to blow his breath toward people. He had his own style or bag of tricks. Sometimes with age, deception is more ingrained.

It's easy when people are in the frame of mind, wanting to fall, and already off balance. When children were prayed for, they could all be made to fall at the same time. It only took one child with falling experience to take them down, with them holding hands. One day a friend of mine told me he was sick of the falling. The man said he would never go back. He recalled his last day at church. He was determined he wouldn't fall. Our pastor was having a hard time trying to make him, and he tried every trick. Finally, he called the man's name and said, "If you won't fall, I'm going to fall." Do you think the preacher was trying to help God make him fall? The man confessed to me, he almost told the preacher, "If you want to fall, go ahead," but he remained silent until the preacher gave up. Neither of them fell; our pastor lied again.

One night our pastor locked hands with his preacher friend. It appeared they were in a power struggle to determine which was the strongest. They slowly went to their knees and gave up. I saw this in the natural when I was a kid. I believe those two were also doing this in the natural or flesh.

God's signs and wonders are far above what false prophets could imagine or conjure up. I don't think God was involved in the nonsense; although it was a big show.

Occasionally, one of them danced in the Spirit. Immediately, the other would begin the same irrational dance. They ran in place as fast as possible, while going around in circles. The preachers thought they were in the Spirit. In my opinion—it wasn't the Holy Spirit. It was the flesh or under the influence of an evil spirit! It ended with exhaustion and they fell. They said if anyone wanted to dance in the Spirit, they missed a good opportunity. Remember our pastor taught, monkey see, monkey do; follow your leader, submit. If you follow men like them, you may be in trouble or worse.

One cool night after a revival episode, two people were active in the parking lot. A lady from our church had a friend visit us. Her friend seemed spiritual; he showed us gold dust in his Bible. I believe it was glitter. He claimed the gold appeared as he attended a well known preacher's crusade. The preacher has a big television ministry. He liked the falling obsession, signs, wonders and of course, money. He is considered by many, a false prophet. I certainly understand why.

Anyway, the two super charged people were taking turns falling in the parking lot while it was pouring rain. The man and woman could not stop laughing and falling down. Spectators from the business next door were enjoying the entertainment. I should've told them what our pastor told the ushers; he declared, "You can control how drunk you get in the Spirit." If God made us drunk in the Spirit, how could man control it? No one controls God!

Meanwhile, at my house during the day, the evangelist and I had some interesting moments. He watched videos of church services where strange things happened among the people. He told me he carefully studied other preachers to discover all he could about the supernatural. He seemed obsessed with the gifts God gives to some. I couldn't get him interested in anything else. It seemed like the evangelist had an addiction; perhaps he did. I hoped for a way to get him out of this obsession. I sincerely tried to help. His response wasn't very nice. Some are offended with anyone's advise.

I decided to play a trick on the evangelist. I wanted him to relax and lighten up. One week before the revival began, our pastor demonstrated the same trick. He asked if we had thought about the upcoming revival. Most everyone raised their hands. Then he asked if God had been dealing with any of us about anything; once again we raised our hands. Immediately, the preacher said these exact words with a loud, cruel voice, "Wrong! God don't make deals; you have been in disobedience!" Was he joking or serious? I believe it was the latter.

When the evangelist began our revival, he pulled the same trick. They probably learned this at Bible college. I reasoned if it was okay for these preachers to display nonsense in church, it would be alright for me to do the same in my home. It seemed like a joke and I like a sense of humor.

My opportunity came, and I couldn't resist. The piano man, evangelist and I were relaxing in my living room. The evangelist was considering moving from Florida to Chicago, Illinois. The preacher went on and on, implying God was dealing with him. I asked, "How long has God been dealing with you about moving?" He replied, "Oh, it's not just me, but it's the whole family." I replied very adamantly, "Wrong! God don't make deals—you have been in disobedience!" The piano man laughed so hard, he almost fell off my sofa. I pointed my finger at the evangelist and said, "I got you, buddy, I gotcha!" I forgot I wasn't supposed to call him buddy. His face turned blood red. Do you remember the saying, he can dish it out, but he can't take it?

I believe the evangelist developed unforgiveness toward me. Please Sir, for your sake, forgive me. I'm sure you'll read this. I mean you no harm. Will you ask your family to read this, and pray about your style of preaching? They know you well and I'm sure they sincerely love you.

Ask them to tell you the truth. The truth will make you free. Jesus said it would. The implication is you have to know the truth to be free. I'll quote Jesus. "And ye shall know the truth, and the truth will make you free." (John 8:32) Please stop the ridiculous show.

Confide in your lovely wife. She knows things you probably can't see yourself. There is an old saying; you don't really know someone until you live with them. It's possible she discerns spirits better than you, especially the ones that trouble you. I'm certain she has your best interest at heart. Everyone needs counsel from someone; even preachers and evangelists. You should be submissive to your wife. Read this in Eph. 5:21.

Please inquire precisely what your wife meant by her eleventh commandment for you, "Thou shalt not fake thyself out." Ask her if she thought you were fake or false. She would know and I'm sure your wife and children are concerned. I love you enough to tell you the truth. You should be honest with yourself and with God.

Jesus Christ declared in Mark 13:22. "...For false Christs and false prophets shall rise, and shall show signs and wonders, to seduce, if it were possible, even the elect." People say, it's impossible for saved people to be deceived or backslide into awful sins without repenting. I think both are possible. Jesus made this plain in Mt. 24:11. "And many false prophets shall rise, and shall deceive many." The seduction of false prophets is directed by the devil and his demons. It's often a slow process, difficult to detect and can happen to anyone!

Human nature tells us—it's always someone else. At times we think there is no way we could be deceived and become a false prophet. Many think they are saved, sealed, delivered, and can do no wrong. Deception knows no boundaries. Jesus made it plain that anyone could be deceived, and that many will. Sometimes we think we're intelligent, even when we do things that are ridiculous.

The standard we should live by is God's Word. This cannot be replaced by religious traditions. If we fail to study the Bible and do what it declares, we may be ruined by false teachings. "...That we henceforth be no more children, tossed to and fro, and carried about with every wind of doctrine, by the sleight of men, and cunning craftiness, whereby they lie in wait to deceive; But speaking the truth in love, may grow up into him in all things, which is the head, even Christ:" (Eph. 4:14–15)

I have a burden for the lost and realize I have to work out my own salvation with fear and trembling. God's Word teaches this. It troubles me, people will live forever in the wrong place. I have a special concern for preachers and teachers. They lead many in the wrong direction, including themselves. Teachers, will be held to a higher standard. Our punishment is going to be more severe if we teach God's Word wrong. The cautions in the Bible written to saints, apply to all the saved people. As a teacher I have a responsibility to study, rightly divide, interpret and teach God's Word correctly. "Look to yourselves, that we lose not those things we have wrought, but that we receive a full reward." (2 John 1: 8)

"Christ is become of no effect to you, whosoever of you are justified by the law; ye are fallen from grace." (Gal. 5:4) Trying to earn salvation with good merits or works will cause anyone to fall from grace. Some think it's impossible to fall from grace. The Bible is full of scriptures that imply we can. Many follow wrong traditions instead of studying their Bible.

Many ways seem correct, but the end result is our death. It never ceases to amaze me how people get into evil without realizing what they are doing. I have done that. We hear God's Word and then fail to do it. In the false prophet's own words, the Word won't work—if you don't work the Word.

CHAPTER EIGHT

MY PASTOR GETS MEANER

W hen a preacher is on the wrong track—he is destined for failure. If he doesn't fail in this life, and repent, he will fail in the next life. Failure is an excellent opportunity to see the light and change. That is what repent means, change and proceed in the right direction. If we don't repent in this life, there is no opportunity for repentance.

The way we live seals our fate for eternity. Everyone's works will be judged... "For we must all appear before the judgment seat of Christ; that everyone may receive the things done in his body, according to that he hath done, whether it be good or bad." (2 Cor. 5:10) A person's death seals their testimony; it cannot be changed.

Our pastor was trying to control the wealthy who attended our church. He didn't see his actions as control. Preachers must love people, and be submissive—if they expect it in return. We have to earn respect. The man should have known Rom. 2:4. "...not knowing that the goodness of God leadeth thee to repentance?" He wouldn't listen. It was very rare that I rebuked my pastor. It was always done with a spirit of meekness and love. The man was rebuked harshly in the past; he wouldn't accept it from anyone. He said he would permit a rebuke by someone above, but not under him. He said, "A rebuke should come from the top down and not from the bottom up." In essence, we shouldn't rebuke him.

The college founder where our pastor attended, wrote many books. I read in one of them, he wanted someone to tell him if he was wrong. He didn't say anything about them being higher or lower. I certainly want advise when I'm wrong—if it's constructive.

We visited many people, inviting them to church. They were bothered by other denominations and cults, so they didn't trust anyone. Our efforts, in daily routines were more effective and less offensive, than groups going door to door. If a preacher walks in love and follows God's Word, a church grows. Members tell others about their church, without knocking on doors. Something caused visitors to leave. It was no surprise to me; our pastor confessed he might be causing people to leave. He was absolutely right and needed to change. The man was confused and struggled with expressing love.

Some accept salvation, and think they don't have to repent anymore. There are cautions for Christians. "Wherefore let him that thinketh he standeth, take heed lest he fall." (1 Cor. 10:12) We are not infallible. When we're walking close with God, pride can develop and deceive us into falling. I've made this mistake and it humbled me. It causes shame and makes us feel degraded. We must stay humble. Please look at these biblical warnings carefully. God won't leave us, but we can leave Him! He will knock on our heart's door; will we let Him in?

A well known TV preacher declared, "If a church won't grow after it has been established for several years, there is a problem at the top." We knew who was at the top of our church. Our pastor knew and seemed proud of that fact. It was pride that caused him many problems and led to his fall; pride will ruin anyone. It caused his church to fail.

We can't correct our faults, when we don't see them. This dilemma is called, denial. When we fail to recognize a problem, we'll probably blame it on someone else. Hard core addicts often blame their problems on everyone else. Our pastor was a hard core controller. Former pastors controlled him, influencing him to develop the same problem. We tend to hurt others with the same hurts we've experienced.

My pastor declared, "If someone controls others, they are committing the sin of witchcraft." I believe that teaching. The works of the flesh are revealed in Galatians chapter five. Witchcraft is listed as a work of the flesh. Controlling people is a simple form of witchcraft. They that do the works of the flesh shall not inherit the kingdom of God. (Gal. 5:19–21 paraphrased) Christians must walk in the Spirit and not the flesh. "For he that soweth to his flesh shall of the flesh reap corruption; but he that soweth to the Spirit shall of the Spirit reap life everlasting. And let us not be weary in well doing: for in due season we shall reap, if we faint not." (Gal. 6:8–9) Notice, the word if makes this a conditional promise.

The Atmosphere Was Charged With Evil Spirits

One Sunday when our pastor was late, we could tell he was angry. It was obvious his wife was also. The atmosphere was charged with evil spirits. The pastor couldn't function until he apologized to his wife. This was refreshing, even though he failed to apologize for being late again. We loved our pastor, overlooked a lot, and hoped he would change. If I hadn't loved my wife so much, I wouldn't have tolerated the ridiculous things we were subjected to.

After blasting us with the same old twenty minute tithing sermon, he wanted two offerings from that point on. New rules surfaced often. I can't remember what the second offering was for. I do remember; it didn't please anyone. People put very little money in.

The preacher said he wanted offerings large enough that an armored car would have to pick them up. Lusting after power and money will ruin anyone. If we put God first, we can handle His gifts; they should be used to help others instead of causing idolatry and lust.

Our pastor thought we were keeping our church from growing. He wanted rid of the wolves before they hurt or killed his sheep. Of course, he didn't suspect himself of being a wolf. I think you can see why I concluded he was. I care enough—to tell him the truth.

Jesus declared, false prophets are wolves in sheep's clothing. It's possible the preacher thought I was a wolf. After all, I certainly didn't do everything he wanted. That wasn't good enough for him. Many have an obsession called—control.

He was afraid to get rid of me, for fear of losing Karen. She was a pillar of the church, well liked and respected. It's possible people thought the same of me. I know they appreciated how I kept the building clean. Our church looked beautiful.

Our pastor used the evangelist in an attempt to make me fully submit. Maybe, he viewed me as a goat. He was taught a goat could be changed. One year later, the plan unfolded and backfired; it was the beginning of the failure of our church. Some churches set things in motion that will inevitably cause their demise. The devil deceives and blinds us. It's time to expose evil without fear of the outcome; I don't fear people. Some can't see mistakes until it's too late. I'm trying my best to correct mine.

Meanwhile, the wolf hunt was on for others. The preacher told me wealthy people were using money to control him. I told him I didn't want to hear it. The people he referred to were more like Jesus than he was. I couldn't understand why he was mean to those people. Perhaps he misunderstood them. They wanted him to keep his promise, allowing a mixture of old hymns with modern praise music.

Some older hymns are anointed and set the tone for praise and worship. God has music in heaven. He may use a balance of both. He probably has music that reaches a higher level than we have. People get upset with others praising God, with different music; it doesn't matter what style. Why do people think their way is always right?

What would be wrong with mixing modern praise and worship with old classic hymns? Do you think it might cause people to praise God on a higher level? Some preach hard about how we get excited at a ball game but not in God's house. Then in contradiction, they won't allow upbeat praise music in their churches.

Many traditions of men and women are horribly wrong but extremely popular. If I chose between popular or making it to heaven, I would choose heaven. It's no surprise some are offended with any subject that pertains to God. Some who call themselves Christians are offended at portions of God's Word. The parts that go against their traditions are overlooked or misinterpreted. We're supposed to live by every word.

It was another fine Sunday morning, we thought. We could tell there was something wrong with our pastor. Suddenly, he went into a rage about the upcoming revival. He pointed out every flaw in our sanctuary. He wanted holes in the walls filled, and everything painted. That project didn't interest me. I was tithing and giving far above that with offerings, time and labor. I was tired, and perhaps experiencing burnout. Often, no one helped me clean the huge building. I tried to give cheerfully, though I was giving more than I could afford.

True: You Can't Out Give God

Often it's been said, you can't out give God. People are correct with that statement. However, it's wrong to use it in defense of someone giving too much. You can give in a wrong way until it hurts. I've been guilty. God knows my heart, obedience, faith, and sacrifices. He really blesses our faith and prefers obedience over sacrifice.

"Now faith is the substance of things hoped for, the evidence of things not seen." (Heb. 11:1) My faith has substance and evidence. I've seen the unseen things of God take on a genuine substance with real evidence. Rom. 1:20 says, "For the invisible things of Him from the creation of the world are clearly seen, being understood by the things that are made, even His eternal power and Godhead; so that they are without excuse." God has placed His laws in our hearts and minds.

Intellectual attempts with good works won't save us. Works are necessary, but can't replace His grace! Good people still have to repent and—ask for His free gift of salvation. Accept Jesus; ask Him for abundant life. We can't please God without faith. The shield of faith will move mountains and stop satanic attacks. Faith is like a vehicle that takes us on our journey. With our faith we see His eternal power and Godhead by things that are made, even His people.

"For as the body without the spirit is dead, so faith without works is dead also." (James 2:26) "Show me thy faith without thy works, and I will show thee my faith by my works." (last part of James 2:18) We are justified by His blood, grace, our faith, works and words. They are necessary! Don't believe part of His Word and deny some of it.

A religious sign stated, Justified by the faith of Christ and not by works. (Gal. 2:16) It left out, of the law. Works or deeds of the law don't justify us; works of faith do. "Knowing that a man is not justified by the works of the law, but by the faith of Jesus Christ, even we have believed in Jesus Christ, that we might be justified by the faith of Christ, and not by the works of the law: for by the works of the law shall no flesh be justified." (Gal. 2:16)

Notice this. "Was not Abraham our father justified by works, when he had offered Isaac his son upon the altar?" (James 2:21) "Likewise also was not Rahab the harlot justified by works, when she had received the messengers, and had sent them out another way?" (James 2:25) "Ye see then how that by works a man is justified, and not by faith only." (James 2:24) We are justified by faith and—works of faith in Jesus Christ. The paraphrase on the sign was wrong and created a falsehood. Pay attention when you read. Most misinterpret the works and salvation doctrines.

Positive Thinking Is Biblical

God's Holy Word declares, "...and shall not doubt in his heart, but shall believe that those things which he saith shall come to pass; he shall have whatsoever he saith..." (Mark 11:23) Jesus expressed a wonderful message. A positive attitude is faith in action and can help us obtain blessings from God. Positive thinking, good works and bearing fruit are biblical. Positive thinking blesses lost people. "...For as he thinketh in his heart, so is he:" (Prov. 23:7) God let thousands die in the wilderness, because of murmuring and complaining! When we're negative, God is not pleased. Stay positive and receive His good gifts.

We need the sincere milk of His precious Word, before we can understand the meat. Milk is for babes in Christ; meat is for mature

Christians. A well balanced person will desire both and we need it all. It takes time, patience and study.

The older evangelist returned for a short revival and he was late. I assisted him with his things. He noticed our pastor was late. The man seemed puzzled with what he was seeing. Have you noticed how keen and observant some preachers are? Sometimes they stare as though they can see right through you. The man asked, "What's going on here?" I said, "We're getting ready for service; come inside." The evangelist hesitated and looked confused. He noticed the small number of vehicles in the parking lot. He asked if this was all the people we had, and what was wrong. It wasn't my place to explain; he could discern for himself.

The evangelist taught his style of witnessing. He didn't ask if someone wanted to accept Jesus; he told them to do this. He acted as if he could force people to get saved. God doesn't work that way and neither can we. There were scare tactics involved. Some preachers use a spirit of fear to lead someone to repentance, "...not knowing that the goodness of God leadeth thee to repentance." (Rom. 2:4) It's the fear of God that helps us live the baptism of repentance!

I'm sure the older evangelist told lies. He declared when he went door to door, ninety to ninety-five percent of the people who needed salvation obtained it. If that was true, why didn't someone follow us back to church for even one visit? The man was exalting himself and he was humbled. He used us to produce false signs and wonders, hoping God would perform real ones. God doesn't need help in this matter.

The End Justifies Any Means—Not True!

He was like other false prophets. Some people think the end justifies the means. The wrong saying could be stated like this; "The end justifies any means." People tell lies—thinking something good will come out of it. You could say: no comment, be silent, or tell the truth in a way that wouldn't hurt. It's dangerous to lie. The evangelist said he would fill our church. It would have taken several hundred people. At that time, we had about a dozen. Gradually, we got back to twenty or thirty. It was no surprise people were suspicious of the little church.

God stopped some of the false prophets in our town. So far as I know, the last one of that group left. Unfortunately, others still exist. False prophets are in all religions.

God allows problems; He knows His grace is sufficient, and His strength is made perfect in weakness. When we are weak, He makes us strong. 2 Cor. 12 explains the sufferings of a Christian. We'll be joint heirs with Jesus, if we suffer with Him. I'm paraphrasing Rom. 8:17.

If there is no resistance we grow weak. Our muscles weaken without resistance. We would weaken spiritually without the problems, trials and troubles. "My brethren, count it all joy when ye fall into divers temptations;" (James 1:2) Blessed are they which are persecuted for righteousness' sake: for theirs is the kingdom of heaven. Blessed are ye, when men shall revile you, and persecute you, and shall say all manner of evil against you falsely for my sake. Rejoice and be exceedingly glad: for great is your reward in heaven: for so persecuted they the prophets which were before you." (Mt. 5:10–12)

Peter wrote, we have fiery trials to test our faith. These problems make us stronger, if we stay close to God. If we don't, they could be more than we can bear.

A man said, "God won't put more temptation on you than you can bear." Another man replied, "I used to believe that, but now I'm not so sure He won't." Both men were wrong. Pay attention to His Word.

The Bible verse they were speaking of is 1 Cor. 10:13. Paul was writing to saved people about common problems. He explains; God is faithful and won't allow more temptation than we can bear. God makes a way of escape so we can overcome our problems. The way of escape is study His Word and pray.

Here is the quote, "There hath no temptation taken you but such as is common to man: but God is faithful, who will not suffer you to be tempted above that ye are able; but will with the temptation also make a way to escape, that ye may be able to bear it." (1 Cor. 10:13) If we don't stay close to God, it's possible we may not bear it. Suffer means allow. God allows temptation, but the devil is the tempter. (Mt. 4:3) Why would He teach against sin, then tempt us to sin?

Most people leave out the word suffer or allow when they refer to 1 Cor. 10:13. By making this mistake, they're implying God places temptation on us. Perhaps we need another verse to confirm this. (James 1:13) "Let no man say when he is tempted, I am tempted of God: for God cannot be tempted with evil, neither tempteth He any man:"

A man said, God put cancer on him, to help him quit smoking. He thought God put sugar diabetes on him, to stop his drinking. God doesn't go against His Word; we will for sure reap what we sow. God's Word is His will. If we don't know God's Word, we can't do His will. How could we pray effectively, fervently and become righteous? Do you think we could avail much? We should know something is right, because it lines up with His Word.

It's easy to create a commandment and teach it as a doctrine of Christ. The false teaching would be like this: It isn't always God's will to heal. Our Heavenly Father allows things that no one understands. Perhaps God allows a bad situation to protect us from a worse state. I don't pretend to know everything; no one does. I do know the scripture must be fulfilled. "Be not deceived; God is not mocked; for whatsoever a man soweth, that shall he also reap." (Gal. 6:7)

If an alcoholic destroyed their liver by excessive drinking, prayed in faith for healing and got it, would they reap what they sowed? They might consider the healing as an excuse for more drinking. They wouldn't learn from their mistakes. This could apply to other sins. We're confident of heaven, with a new body that lives forever with no pain!

If we don't receive healing from God, we shouldn't blame Him. More than likely, it's our fault. The Bible declares this, "...For all have sinned, and come short of the glory of God;" (Rom. 3:23) "For the wages of sin is death..." (Rom. 6:23)

It is God's will to heal. However, God doesn't always get His will. God gave us free will. Here is a classic example in 2 Peter 3:9. The last part of the verse explains this. "...The Lord is not slack concerning His promise, as some men count slackness; but is long-suffering to us-ward, not willing that any should perish, but that all should come to repentance." God wants everyone to accept Him, but it's our choice. That is love my friend! God doesn't control us into His heaven.

Here is another example of a false teaching. God gave Paul a thorn in the flesh. He said it was a messenger of Satan sent to buffet him, but some think it was a sickness, to help him. Remember, I am listing false teachings!

God put cancer on Uncle Henry so his horrible suffering would cause Aunt Sally to accept Jesus. They said their child didn't accidentally run in front of the truck. They said God needed him—so He took him. Wait a minute, does God need anything? Does the Bible verify He does? God is in control of most things. God lets us control some things! He knows what He is doing, doesn't make any mistakes and doesn't control our free will! He wants us to learn from our mistakes and ask for His help.

Here are more false teachings. He made my wife go crazy after the loss of our child. God knew if she lost her mind, we would draw closer to Him. I know Joe is a good man but when his wife left, he is no longer qualified to preach, even though he did nothing wrong.

Fred is divorced, not by choice. Since he remarried, he should stop preaching because he isn't the husband of one wife. The law says, he is the husband of one wife, but I'm sure God doesn't see it that way, because of our traditions. Wake up; divorce is not the un-pardonable sin. The husband of one wife qualification is misinterpreted. Churches lose qualified preachers and deacons because of it. If we have erred on these things, what else are we wrong about? I want to know how and why we have been so wrong. There is a way to correct our mistakes.

We can be so anointed with the Holy Spirit that we have no need of being taught. This can be found in the books of 1 Cor. 2: 13–16 and 1 John 2:27. However, we should remain teachable. Many Bible verses imply that and it's not a contradiction!

If God hadn't given us free will to make our own choices, good or bad, we wouldn't have learned anything. God loves us very much; He lets us do whatever we want. *Thank you Father for not controlling us. Help us to be more like you and love the way you do. I ask in the name of Jesus Christ.*

He knew we would sin and see the need for a Savior. God pleads with us in many ways. He speaks through His creation: wind, rain, teachers, preachers, His Word, TV, radio, His Spirit, and our conscience.

Atheists pretend they don't believe in God. Deep down, they do. We should look at Rom. 1:19–20. It explains how and why everyone knows about God. Please don't wait; accept Jesus. The Bible declares, "...Now is the day of salvation." (2 Cor. 6:2) We make one of two choices and it is our decision! Indecision is the wrong choice. Behold, now is the accepted time—not later.

Believers with faith can pray and get protection from a storm. We do not stop the storm, but God will honor our prayer. God controls the weather. If we could, everyone would have different weather; what chaos we would have. We can't control the earth's orbit around the sun and how the universe works. Free will means—we can choose Him!

A thrill seeker is asking for trouble. One slight mistake and they could be killed. They would be in control, unless God prevented it. "Jesus said unto him, it is written again, thou shalt not tempt the Lord thy God." (Mt. 4:7) Remember, God is tempted by no man; don't even try it. I loved my earthly father and feared him; I fear God even more.

Some only hear God's Word occasionally at church. Most sermons I've heard don't contain much of God's Word. Wrong traditions are the main topics of these lectures. Everything spoken from a pulpit doesn't come from God. People make mistakes. If no one stands up for what is right, evil prevails. We must return to the old fashioned Bible studies, where everyone can participate and learn the truths about God.

Some worship people more than their Creator. Some might worship their church building. Some idols are made of wood and stone. Why do we become so wrapped up in the stuff of this world? Our life is but a vapor that is over in a moment, compared with eternity. We should not become so worldly; there is another world out there—a paradise in heaven. All troubles will be gone: no more pain, suffering or worry. Stop worshiping things and idolizing people. We make them into false gods, without realizing how dangerous it is. When God declared, thou shalt have no other gods before me—we should take it seriously.

Preachers and teachers make mistakes. Be careful who you follow. Wake up church; we are in the last days nearing the second coming of Jesus Christ. Be listening for the trumpet. Look up; our redemption is coming! Do you know Jesus on a personal level? He is knocking on your heart's door right now. Open your heart and let Him in.

CHAPTER NINE

THE YOUNG WOLF RETURNS

It was revival time again! The revivals were occurring more often. Our pastor's favorite evangelist came to save the day. I was using irony. He didn't help; he hurt us. No doubt, his intentions were good. Most preachers don't do evil intentionally. They're tricked like everyone is.

Invisible beings (spirits) whisper words in our minds. We can assume these are our thoughts. If we don't have enough of God's Word in our hearts, we can act on terrible thoughts. Some call this deceived by the devil. In essence it is, because evil spirits are under the devil's influence.

The devil can't be everywhere, like God is. He sends demons to harass us. (1 John 4:4) "...greater is He that is in you, than he that is in the world." We can have power over evil spirits with the name of Jesus.

Demons are fallen angels that lived in heaven long ago. It's possible after they sinned and were thrown out, they felt miserable and wanted others to share in their misery. By causing people to sin and be in the same dilemma, they may not feel as bad. They might boast, "We're not so bad, look at these others who are like us." There is an old saying: misery loves company.

People do this as well. Those who are deep in sin bring others down to their level. Perhaps it makes them feel better about themselves. The more they influence others to sin, the more it seems alright or normal. Some people actually believe they'll have a party in hell with their friends. That is sad; the Bible describes it as the opposite.

Before I explain the revival, I need to tell about the loss of a friend. When the devil knows a friendship will cause his kingdom hurt or loss, he attacks. The attacks came through people talking trash. Even my friend was deceived. It was told, I was playing games on my friend. When games are played on someone, deceit is used. This is called lying. I'm aware of the fact, all liars will have their part in the lake of fire. I try my best to love and help people. Most arguments are trivial. Others were gossiping and upset my friend. I saw clearly; our friendship wasn't going to last. When people aren't compatible and there is already friction between them, it's best to dissolve the friendship. It will help others stop their gossip.

As the revival began, it was obvious the attendance was down. There was a quiet sadness among the congregation. The evangelist knew how to liven up the services and cause laughter. He enjoyed watching the dignified businessman rolling on the floor and laughing. Sure, I was tempted to do the same, but managed to refrain. Emotions can cause us to dishonor God. At times emotionalism isn't spiritual!

The preacher made fun of people and got too personal. One man told me, he didn't appreciate being called the town drunk. His problem was in his past and didn't escalate to that level. The preacher embarrassed others to make himself appear discerning and important. Of course the evangelist thought God gave him a gift of insight, into peoples' lives. The word of knowledge is a spiritual gift, but it can be misused.

The Bible informs, "A merry heart doeth good like a medicine." (Prov. 17:22) Laughing at a person's past won't help them. Some were hurt severely and aren't over it. Some forget how fragile people can be.

Our pastor and the evangelist, tried to cheer up everyone. They wanted people to bring in visitors. We didn't have our hearts in it. The Spirit of God was hindered; something was wrong. The preachers thought it was our fault. I suppose we were confused. Confusion is not of God; it's of the devil. "For God is not the author of confusion, but of peace, as in all churches of the saints." (1 Cor. 14:33) James 3:16 made it plain. "For where envying and strife is, there is confusion and every evil work." The preachers, were full of envy, strife and control. We were brainwashed, and didn't realize it.

They were determined to remove people if they wouldn't submit. Nothing was working right in our church. It had been a long time since anyone accepted Jesus Christ as Lord and Savior. Salvation should be the main focus in any church: not signs, wonders and glory for ourselves. People in churches make similar mistakes. They focus on—themselves, policies and their positions. When the focus isn't on love, we don't have Jesus first. Remember the Bible declares, God is love. (1 John 4:8) "He that loveth not knoweth not God; for God is love."

Since large crowds didn't arrive, large amounts of money didn't. The two preachers wanted to keep the revival going another week. They decided instead, to try one month later. As the cruelty of those false prophets increased, the judging had to increase. That was a mission I didn't enjoy, but found necessary.

Jesus declared this. "...I am come that they might have life, and that they might have it more abundantly." (John 10:10) I must do my part to fulfill His will in my life. We must conduct ourselves in a way that we promote long life and abundance. God is pleased that I am willing to give my life; however, His will is, that we live. "Delight thyself also in the Lord; and He shall give thee the desires of thine heart." (Ps. 37:4) The effectual, fervent prayer of a righteous man avails much.

If I pray according to His will and don't doubt in my heart whatever I ask Him, I shall have those things. I am paraphrasing James 5:16 and Mark 11:23. The previous verses are enormous faith builders. Actually God's Word is where faith is obtained. "So then faith cometh by hearing, and hearing by the word of God." (Rom. 10:17)

Well meaning people take a verse or two from the Bible, and create numerous false doctrines. Sometimes the teachings sound okay, but aren't logical. The things of God aren't always common sense or simple. Our Father's ways are extraordinary and supernatural.

God declared this. "...so are my ways higher than your ways and my thoughts than your thoughts." (Isaiah 55:9) The Bible says, "...comparing spiritual things with spiritual." (1 Cor. 2:13) In other words, we must compare scriptures with scriptures to understand the Bible. We should live by every word. This won't happen without Bible study. We are instructed to study to show ourselves approved to God, a worker that doesn't have to be ashamed, because of correctly interpreting God's Word. I just explained 2 Tim. 2:15.

The Bible warns what happens if we add to and take away from His Word. Pastors and teachers paraphrase when they interpret or explain scriptures. They can accomplish this, without adding to and taking away from the words. Misinterpreting the Bible is perilous and so is teaching from an inferior translation. Let us receive wisdom from Ecclesiastes chapter three. "To everything there is a season, and a time to every purpose under the heaven:

A time to be born, and a time to die;

A time to plant, and a time to pluck up that which is planted;

A time to kill, and a time to heal;

A time to break down, and a time to build up;

A time to weep, and a time to laugh;

A time to mourn, and a time to dance;

A time to cast away stones,

and a time to gather stones together;

A time to embrace, and a time to refrain from embracing;

A time to get, and a time to lose;

A time to keep, and a time to cast away;

A time to rend, and a time to sew;

A time to keep silence, and a time to speak;

A time to love, and a time to hate;

A time of war, and a time of peace."

There is a time for almost everything. "Thou shalt not kill," doesn't contradict, "A time to kill." Thou shalt not kill refers to murder, an unlawful killing. A time to kill refers to justifiable homicide, self-defense, and in the defense of one's country.

When we think the Bible contradicts itself—we are misinterpreting. Misinterpreting God's Word is dangerous. It's taking away from the words of the Bible. Some know Rev. 22:19, which warns what will happen if we take away from the words. Many don't fully comprehend or properly interpret that scripture. That verse should be revealed as we compare scriptures with other scriptures and live by all of God's Word.

The Bible teaches how we should not judge others. In other places, it tells us how to judge. Here are examples of appropriate judging. (1 Cor. 10:15) "I speak as to wise men; judge ye what I say." (1 Cor. 11:31) "For if we would judge ourselves, we should not be judged." (1 Cor. 14:29) "Let the prophets speak two or three, and let the other judge..." (1 Cor. 6:1–5) "Dare any of you, having a matter against another, go to law before the unjust, and not before the saints? Do ye not know that the saints shall judge the world? And if the world shall be judged by you, are ye unworthy to judge the smallest matters? Know ye not that we shall judge angels? How much more things that pertain to this life? If then ye have judgments of things pertaining to this life, set them to judge who are least esteemed in the church. I speak to your shame. Is it so, that there is not a wise man among you? No, not one that shall be able to judge between his brethren?" (1 Cor. 2:15–16) "But he that is spiritual judgeth all things, yet he himself is judged of no man. For who hath known the mind of the Lord, that he may instruct Him? But we have the mind of Christ."

Many look for excuses to believe their wrong traditions. Some wouldn't believe what Paul wrote in First Corinthians about judging. They only believe Jesus. In John 7:24 Jesus explained this. "Judge not according to the appearance, but judge righteous judgment." In Luke 7:43 Jesus told Peter, "Thou hast rightly judged." Jesus said, "I judge no man." (John 8:15) He meant, I condemn no man, which lines up with John 3:17. "For God sent not his Son into the world to condemn the world; but that the world through him might be saved." In John 8:26 Jesus declares, "I have many things to say and to judge of you:" Jesus and Paul explained how we should judge and how we shouldn't. Please judge my writings with God's Word. (in the right way)

Isn't it obvious there is a right and wrong way to judge people? Words can have different meanings. Sometimes they are opposite. Pride and fear have opposite meanings. The Bible reveals in many places to fear God. The

Bible explains, we should fear not. Our Heavenly Father has not given us a spirit of fear. However, He expects us to fear Him. Some fear their earthly father; we should fear our Heavenly Father—more. As we study the Bible, the so-called contradictions disappear.

There are words that have a few short definitions. It's amazing how each of these are almost identical. Whereby is a good example: by what, how, by which. It means how or the way. It doesn't mean because, like some think. Some words only mean one thing. Teachers and preachers should be careful what they say. We should know what we are talking about and what words mean!

Please consider the word grieve. It doesn't mean disappoint. It means intense sorrow. Please read the short verse in Ephesians chapter four, verse thirty. Having an accurate interpretation of this short sentence will help us realize, we've misinterpreted many scriptures. This verse is key to understanding the most important doctrines. This short study changed my life and helped me realize false prophets have used traditions to confuse us. Jesus said, "And ye shall know the truth, and the truth shall make you free." (John 8:32)

Some people say we shouldn't judge anyone, anywhere, anytime. The fact is, we have to judge people in the right way—often. Let me give a couple examples of—appropriate judging. If you needed a baby-sitter, you would check references and do a background check. You judged them—good for you. If the sitter beat your children almost to death, you would judge them and press charges. The saying, "we aren't supposed to judge anyone" isn't scripturally correct.

Traditions can become a religion that needs a lot to be desired; it's dangerous. Jesus spoke harshly to the scribes and Pharisees about their traditions of men! Beware of wrong teachings from our modern day Pharisees. They reside in every religion.

God has chosen, called and prepared me to do some judging. He knew I would do it with love and the proper motive. My motive is to lead people to Jesus Christ and heaven. I can think of nothing better to do. It sure would be nice to lay up treasures in heaven. Jesus Christ told us to. We can't take money or possessions to heaven, only people. They are treasures and we should treat them as such!

Some have a form of godliness, but deny the power thereof; from such we should turn away. (paraphrasing 2 Tim. 3:5) Beware of people who say God doesn't do miracles through people.

God chose the evangelist Billy Graham to lead thousands, if not millions, to Jesus Christ for their salvation. Even false prophets admit salvation is the best miracle. In the past and future, millions of people have and will lead others to Jesus. Thank God for His grace and free gift of salvation. Thank God for people who lead us to Jesus for that gift! We aren't to rejoice because we have power over evil spirits, but because our names are written in heaven. (paraphrasing Luke 10:20) We should keep the main thing—salvation, our focus.

When a doctor performs brain surgery after his colleagues say it's impossible, they call it a miracle. God and the doctor should get credit. "Every good gift and every perfect gift is from above, and cometh down from the Father of lights." (James 1:17) When we do anything good, we should always thank God and give Him the credit.

"My people are destroyed for lack of knowledge..." (Hosea 4:6) Some don't believe God heals today. They believe doctors can, and don't realize they are good gifts. They don't understand that every good thing is from God. The Bible says God is good. His mercy endures forever, appears in His Word more than thirty times. Some use that as an excuse to sin.

Some believe God can heal, but sometimes won't, to teach someone a lesson. They say God places sickness on a person to help them or someone else. Some believe God controls everything, does bad things and is responsible for everything that happens. God is omnipotent and He rules the universe with all power. He knows everything including the future. He can do anything, except in the areas He chooses not to. God allowed humanity to fall. (sin) He didn't want us to have knowledge of good and evil, but he allowed it. It wasn't His will. He allowed sin but didn't promote it. God knew He would help us overcome through the blood of his Son. Jesus will help, if we believe and follow Him. "Blessed are they that do his commandments, that they may have right to the tree of life, and may enter in through the gates into the city." (Rev. 22:14) Obeying Jesus Christ is following Him; it is imperative.

Some believe Jesus came to kill, steal and destroy. That sounds like a kingdom divided against itself. Jesus declared this. "Every kingdom divided against itself is brought to desolation..." (Mt. 12:25) People have to decide for themselves; is God good or not?

Heb. 12:2 says, Jesus is the author and finisher of our faith. Some think we don't have to do anything because of this scripture. He is the Creator of all things, even our faith. He helps us finish this race, or salvation journey, but He won't do for us, what He commands us to do.

We can't do things on our own. Jesus said, without me you can do nothing. If anyone thinks we don't have to do anything, they need to study works in the Bible. Pay close attention to the works of faith. Faith without works doesn't exist; it's dead. True faith contains works; we find that in James 2:17–18. Here are three of my favorite verses. "For by grace are ye saved through faith; and that not of yourselves: it is the gift of God: Not of works, lest any man should boast. For we are his workmanship, created in Christ Jesus unto good works, which God hath before ordained that we should walk in them." (Eph. 2:8–10) Of means—derived from. Salvation is of and by God's free gift, grace. It's not of ourselves or works but through our works. We are saved by grace through the works of faith in Jesus Christ. There is no other or easier way, though many think so.

Some say salvation is by God's grace, through His grace, plus or minus nothing. That sounds like a half truth. Often a half truth is a lie. By grace through faith—we are saved. Work out your own salvation with fear and trembling! This truth is found in the last part of Phil. 2:12. Jesus told His disciples, "If ye keep my commandments, ye shall abide in my love; even as I have kept my Father's commandments, and abide in his love." (John 15:10) It takes effort to follow Jesus. When Jesus said bear fruit, He meant do good deeds. He did His part; will we do ours?

Our Faith Is Counted For Righteousness

Jesus taught in the Great Commission, "They shall lay hands on the sick, and they shall recover." It's true it won't work without faith. It's our faith that is counted for righteousness. Our righteousness must exceed that of some religious people or we won't enter heaven. We confirm that statement by what Jesus declared in Mt. 5:20. "For I say unto you, that except your righteousness shall exceed the righteousness of the scribes and Pharisees, ye shall in no case enter into the kingdom of heaven." It should be crystal clear; we have to do some things.

Someone that needs healing needs faith. Apostle Paul prayed for a man after he perceived—he had faith for healing. If the blind lead the blind, they both fall into a ditch. In other words, a person with no faith praying for someone with no faith won't work. James knew what faith was. The effectual, fervent, prayer of a righteous man avails much. (paraphrasing James 5:14–16)

Have we considered, maybe we're doing something wrong? What about lack of faith? Do you think doubt, fear or unbelief is a problem? "But the fearful, and unbelieving, and the abominable, and murders, and whoremongers, and sorcerers, and idolaters, and all liars, shall have their part in the lake which burneth with fire and brimstone: which is the second death." (Rev. 21:8) The Bible declares, ...It is high time to awake out of your sleep... I am paraphrasing Rom. 13:11. The unbelieving end up in hell. Having faith in God is fundamental and necessary!

A Sunday School teacher said there was a ten day time period between the ascension of Jesus and the outpouring of the Holy Ghost on the day of Pentecost. He claimed God gave special power to some, only for this ten-day period. I'm sure he was referring to miracle working power done through people, in the name of Jesus. After the teacher taught this, he had someone read this verse. (Acts 1:8) "But ye shall receive power, after that the Holy Ghost is come upon you: and ye shall be witnesses unto Me both in Jerusalem, and in all Judea, and in Samaria, and unto the uttermost part of the earth." The power came after people received the baptism of the Holy Ghost.

Paul, Peter, Phillip and Stephen did many signs, wonders, and miracles as God anointed them. This was a long time after the ascension of Jesus and the ten days thereafter! Don't deny the power of God. People don't understand certain baptisms. Satan didn't create anything; he can't. God created all things, languages, tongues and baptisms.

People can have this power in the name of Jesus, if God wills. God is the same yesterday, today, and forever. He doesn't keep good things from His children. We fail to receive them because of unbelief and wrong traditions. Paul told Timothy to keep the traditions. (good ones)

It's the saddest thing to see someone have many health problems. They should trust God to help them. I realize some can't help it. Sometimes we aren't healed and can't understand why. Keep the faith and hang in there. If we aren't healed in this life, we will be in heaven! *Thank you Father for a new body with no more pain, in Jesus name.*

I prayed for a woman who was injured in a car wreck. She felt movement in her spine and got excited when she received healing. Prior to this, her faith was increased through my prayers and counsel, in the name of Jesus Christ. Incredible peace came on her. Before I left, she looked fifteen years younger. She was lively and happy. It's great what God does for us in the name of Jesus.

We agreed in prayer that her home would sell quickly so she could move to New Jersey with friends. I thought it was a done deal, and she must have shared the same faith. I met her realtor soon after and asked if the property sold. She gave me a big smile and a high five. The house sold quickly and for full price. The realtor told me the woman was very happy and looked ten years younger. I said, "No, she looked fifteen years younger!" I told her about praying in the name of Jesus. I could see excitement all over her face as she proclaimed, "I believe it!"

When someone sows the Word of God in your heart, Satan comes immediately and takes it away. (paraphrasing Mark 4:15) We don't have to allow this, but sometimes it only takes a simple distraction, and it's gone. We must fill our heart with His Word. "Thy word is a lamp unto my feet, and a light unto my path." (Ps. 119:105)

The devil steals the Word in other ways. Through traditions of men he instructs; that scripture is not for today; that verse was done away with; speaking in tongues is from the devil; God doesn't heal today and He doesn't do miracles anymore! The lies he puts in people's minds go on without end.

Let me explain what is from the devil—anything that doesn't line up with the Word of God. If you've never read a Bible, you still know what is right and wrong. (Heb. 10:16) "...This is the covenant that I will make with them after those days, saith the Lord, I will put my laws into their hearts, and in their minds will I write them;" We know what to do! God reveals Himself and His laws to everyone. We have no excuse for not obeying God. Whosoever will, can follow and obey Jesus. (be saved)

Some people think they have good reasons for not accepting God's salvation, and maybe He will excuse them. I'm sorry for them; they are deceived by the devil. He uses many forms of deception and he is a liar.

Many believe if God is so good, He won't send people to a place called hell. They think the Bible contradicts itself on this and many other subjects. If we believe that, we're misinterpreting. Hell was prepared for the devil and his angels. It's not God's will that we go there.

There are many reasons God is good. One of them is because He believes in punishment. Discipline or chastising is punishment. It can bring forth the peaceable fruit of righteousness. Read about this in Hebrews chapter twelve. You'll see, if you love your children, you will punish them when necessary. God loves his children and does the same. Do you remember when your parents punished you? It caused you to do right. If we weren't disciplined, we wouldn't be as good as we are. Without laws and law enforcement we would have total disorder. Without jails and prisons where would the incentive be to do right? I think you can see, God is still good, even though He punishes.

It's the goodness of the Lord that draws men to repentance. It's the love and fear of God that keeps some on the straight and narrow path that leads to eternal life. Fear of hell causes some people to repent.

Hell is a bad place, no doubt. In another way of looking at it—it's a guarantee. Hell is necessary because punishment is essential. "...It is a fearful thing to fall into the hands of the living God." (Heb. 10:31) If we don't believe God is good, we're denying His Word and Him. Don't deny Jesus, or He will deny you. "But whosoever shall deny me before men, him will I also deny before my Father which is in heaven." (Mt. 10:33)

We should strengthen our faith. If it isn't strong, we may fail the tests of life. Don't wait until horrible things come your way; they will. Use the armor of God to fight evil. It's truth, righteousness, the gospel, salvation, His Word, prayer, and of course faith. We must above all things, use our shield of faith to protect us from the attacks of the devil and evil spirits. God helps those who obey Him!

CHAPTER TEN

THE REVIVAL FROM HELL

It was a month later, and the evangelist returned. He preached revivals around the world. Why would he travel to a small town, to a church with thirty people? Before the revival was over, he was probably wondering why.

Our pastor asked me to measure the front of the church. He was preparing to buy carpet and padding; he wanted it installed before the revival. I measured the front to the first pew as requested. When the carpet arrived, it wasn't enough. The pad was installed when we realized there wasn't enough carpet or padding. I called my pastor and he said forget about the installation.

I volunteered to drive to Georgia that night and pick up what we needed. He didn't like the idea, until I told him I would pay for everything. Late the next day, I arrived with twice as much carpet as he wanted. It covered the front and past the pews. My friends helped install everything and place the furniture and sound system back in perfect order.

Our pastor picked up the evangelist at the airport. He put his friend in a motel close to him, so they could have fellowship time before each night's service. We were having another week long revival.

I worked hard to make sure the revival went smoothly. We didn't dream of having the problems that were about to happen. I thought our church was okay. I loved everyone and thought they loved me.

We enjoyed fellowship with our church family. One lady built a fire in her yard and roasted hotdogs. Karen and I had pool parties, cookouts and baptizing services. The pastor's wife took pictures of everyone. I'm sure she had a church photo album. I wondered if these photos were used to convey who was doing what, when and where. This could be used to inform the evangelist. The man could envision or pretend to receive a word of knowledge from God. He could reveal shocking things about us that supposedly, only God knew. This would build faith for greater miracles and healings. We can't manipulate God!

I know why our pastor needed this fellowship time. Remember the wicked saying, the end justifies the means? No, the end doesn't justify any means, especially evil. Tricks, deception and lies should never be used, thinking something good will happen.

A woman told me she revealed to the evangelist in confidence, that her son had a drug problem. During a service, the preacher called the young man a drug addict, in a degrading way. I viewed the incident as inexcusable. After they exchanged ugly comments, the preacher implied God revealed this to him. The evangelist was just like our pastor; he told lies. Many tell lies and believe they are justified. This is sad. Perhaps they think the end justifies the means.

The young man and his mother were hurt. He asked his mother if she told the evangelist about his drug problem. She lied to him and said "no." She died about two years later. "...The goodness of God leadeth thee to repentance." (Rom. 2:4) Some preachers think they can use rudeness to make people repent. God doesn't work that way, and neither should we.

He Had Been In Fights At Other Churches

After the revival, the young man wanted to fight the evangelist. I'm glad he kept his composure. The way those two preachers behaved, they would have enjoyed a fight. The evangelist told us—he had been in fights at other churches. He seemed pleased as he bragged about having a black belt in karate. He told us the ugly names he was called in other churches. In hindsight, I believe the names were appropriate. The man wasn't nice and obviously, he was deceived.

I spoke with a lady about how she was made a spectacle, during one of the first services. The preacher pointed his finger at her and shouted in a repulsive way, "Woman you have been involved in a relationship with a man and it will destroy you! You need to stop now!"

I asked her if a certain friend was aware of this improper relationship. She said yes. I said, "Please reason with me. Don't you think his rebuke should have been done in private?" She said, "Yes, I do." I said, "Since God knows the future and knew the preacher would embarrass you, do you believe God revealed this information to him?" She didn't believe God revealed it. I said, "Since your friend was always talking to our pastor, don't you think it's possible she told him, and he relayed it to the evangelist?" She suspected this was true.

I wasn't guessing; I was doing some detective work. At times we need to find the motives of those who teach and preach. I promise God will be the ultimate judge. I discovered the woman not only revealed the information to her friend, but also to our pastor. It's possible, instead of this being a word of knowledge, it was a word of gossip.

The woman's friend was the same one I wrote about several chapters earlier. She was one of the main women who organized our church. The woman was always on her phone and she often spoke with our pastor. She put too much confidence in him.

The evangelist preached hard about what happens to people who are not submissive. It was obvious, a hard push was being orchestrated to make people do what they wanted. He explained, people who tried to control pastors with their wealth, would lose money, get divorced, and lose their businesses. Scare tactics don't work well, especially in church. The Bible explains, we don't have to fear false prophets. (Deut. 18:22)

I hope the preachers realize what they are, before it's too late. I hope they repent and restore their salvation, along with the older evangelist. I feel sure all three of these preachers don't believe in once saved, always saved. Some people have lost the fear of God, or never had it.

A man was confused; the evangelist tried to make him fall. He resisted the preacher's efforts and tried to get away. The evangelist forced the man to the floor and placed his Bible on his stomach. He put his foot on the Bible and pushed forcefully several times, saying, "Ha-Ha, Ho-Ho, Hee-Hee." I didn't think it was humorous and neither did the man. He often used these words to make others laugh. I hadn't noticed him pushing on someone's abdomen before. The man winced with pain. He told me after he quit the church, the preacher hurt him.

The man confessed to me two years after he quit, his mind wasn't right because of the brainwashing. I told him I knew exactly how he felt. The man was confined to an institution for a long time. He struggles to this day. Shame on you false prophets, you wolves in sheep's clothing! How is this worshiping God, or helping anyone?

A woman requested prayer for hearing loss in one of her ears. After the evangelist prayed, he had me hold my finger on her good ear, so he could test the defective one. He stood behind her and snapped his fingers twice. Then he asked her to do the same. She snapped her fingers twice. It was impressive, with his microphone amplifying everything. Later, I thought about his trick. She had enough hearing in her good ear to hear the snap, even though it was covered. Later, the woman admitted her ear wasn't healed. It's no surprise; God doesn't honor or reward such sinful behavior. Punishment is the word that comes to my mind.

Jesus declared this, "For false Christs and false prophets shall rise, and shall show signs and wonders, to seduce, if it were possible, even the elect." (Mark 13:22) Matthew wrote, Jesus said the very elect. It's a fact; we were saved but deceived.

A nice man requested prayer for severe pain in his abdomen. The evangelist wouldn't pray for him because he was angry. I asked the man why the preacher was angry. He had questioned the evangelist about something that was wrong. The preacher viewed him as his enemy.

Before the last service was over, the evangelist and my pastor viewed me as their enemy. This came as a complete shock. It was as if they hated me. I wasn't mean or disrespectful, it was the total submission that had me confused. I was troubled, and the false preachers weren't the ones who could help.

It's difficult to recall everything that happened in the revival. I've tried to recall the worst events. We try to forget when horrible things happen. I believe it's a normal thing, possibly a protection device God provides, to help us heal from emotional wounds. I'll ask God to remove this loss of memory. Hopefully, I can reveal things others need to know, to avoid pain and suffering. No one should have to endure what we did. If you are in a bad church, get out!

God can turn bad experiences into good. "Likewise the Spirit also helpeth our infirmities: for we know not what we should pray for as we ought: but the Spirit itself maketh intercession for us with groanings which cannot be uttered. And he that searcheth the hearts knoweth what is the mind of the Spirit, because he maketh intercession for the saints according to the will of God. And we know that all things work together for good to them that love God, to them who are the called according to his purpose." (Rom. 8:26–28) Look at how His Spirit was praying.

Which Spirit of God prays for us? "Who is he that condemeth? It is Christ that died, yea rather, that is risen again, who is even at the right hand of God, who also maketh intercession for us." (Rom. 8:34) Jesus prays the perfect will of God in the Spirit. We should study praying in the Spirit and with understanding. Criticize the misuse of tongues—not the gift. Praying in the Spirit was created by God and He created all things. Some preachers condemn something without studying it. Don't teach a subject—you know nothing about! Attempting to verify wrong traditions with a Bible causes many misinterpretations of God's Word.

Early in this revival, good things were revealed about us. The experience was called, a word of knowledge for everyone. Our pastor said, God told the evangelist things about us. In hindsight, I don't think God revealed it. Don't deny the word of knowledge gift; it's biblical. Most gifts are misused. Maybe it was witchcraft or fortune telling. I've heard it called, "reading your mail." Perhaps it was two preachers using the church photo album and gossiping.

Nice comments were made about everyone at first. At the end of the week, we heard appalling statements. Threats were directed toward anyone who might speak against them. We were expected to take care of preachers better than a king. This is absurd, but the two men believed it.

When the evangelist said treat preachers better than a king, our pastor smiled with approval. A scripture was used to verify his statement. A good minister would receive royal treatment. Remember these guys were false. Long ago, false prophets were killed. The Bible declares; they bring upon themselves swift destruction. I'm paraphrasing 2 Peter 2:1. (the last part)

The evangelist told us to not say anything against our preacher, even if he was wrong. He implied the same for himself. He declared the consequences would be horrific. This may be true for good prophets, not false ones. I think you can tell, I'm not afraid. I only fear my Heavenly Father.

The preacher made fun of how we talk. He talked slower than us in a mocking way. Actually, we were nice and accepted his jokes. This time, it was different; we could tell he was angry. The man wasn't joking; he was serious. Something was wrong with the evangelist; he was making fun of us, and our town.

The man said, "I don't know why your pastor would come to this little town; there is nothing here. I know he didn't come here for the money. He had offers from three different churches where he could have made more money. This man has a good job; he doesn't have to put up with your crap!" After a couple more insults, he repeated it. The next time, the man spelled, c-r-a-p and explained, "For those who don't know what that means, it spells CRAP!" He should have known he was wrong about us. We were nice enough to sit there and take his junk!

I don't hate those preachers. "Be ye angry and sin not: let not the sun go down upon your wrath: Neither give place to the devil." (Eph. 4:26–27) When we hate a person, we must get over it quickly and forgive. The Bible teaches, there is a time to love and a time to hate. We should hate the devil and his demons. They were influencing those two men to hurt themselves and our church.

God allows the devil to win some battles, but He will not win in the end. God wins most battles and has certainly won the conflict. Whose side do you want to be on, the winner or loser? The choice is entirely up to you. Please choose Jesus Christ, right now. Don't wait another minute and with sincerity admit you're a sinner. "Sincerely" ask Jesus to save you from your sins. Many don't understand the simplicity of salvation. It's by His grace and through our faith. Call someone if you need help. They would be more than honored to lead you to Jesus Christ. If you don't know who to call, you can always call on God anytime day or night.

I hate to write the ugly word the evangelist used. When the cruelty spewed from his mouth, I glanced at my pastor. He had a big smile on his face. He clearly approved of the nasty language directed at us.

A shepherd is to watch over his flock and protect them. He should, when a wolf arrives to hurt or kill. We have to overlook, forgive and continue to love, even those who struggle with expressing love. People need love, at times—tough love! We must love some from a distance!

About two years prior, our pastor was preaching a sermon. He said, and I quote, "If a visiting preacher in this church says something wrong, I will stop him on the spot and correct him." He lied, unless he really believed we were full of it! We have to walk in love, even in a rebuke.

Galatians 6:1 and 10 say, "Brethren, if a man be overtaken in a fault, ye which are spiritual, restore such a one in the spirit of meekness; considering thyself, lest thou also be tempted. (10) As we have therefore opportunity, let us do good unto all men, especially unto them who are of the household of faith." We should be extra nice to those in church.

Friday night was the final night of the revival. This was supposedly miracle healing night. God won't be someone's puppet and do magic tricks at their command. Faith and obedience pleases God—not deceit.

Many were prayed for, and a variety of healing requests were made. It was almost like the Holy Spirit wasn't there. I didn't see any healings or miracles in that service. The atmosphere seemed saturated with evil and it was. Evil spirits cause this sort of madness and instigate trouble in every way they can. They work through those who don't know their methods of attack. We have to guard our minds when wrong thoughts enter. Think good and positive thoughts; it's biblical!

The evangelist ran all over the building making people fall. Since I couldn't keep up with him, I stopped trying. I stood there numb with disbelief. The reality of this so-called church was beginning to show. We were wrong for supporting this foolishness. Finally, I sat on the front pew in a cloud of shock and sadness. I felt like I was in a horrible nightmare.

Everyone had enough of people falling over others and on top of each other. All the laughing stopped. It was quiet as the evangelist tried to make someone run or dance. He couldn't persuade anybody to run or dance in the Spirit. He pleaded in a helpless way, "Would somebody dance? Would somebody run?" Our pastor came to his friend's rescue. He instructed an usher to dance. His dance looked sad and strange. His grandmother told me later, she wanted to run out of there, but she didn't. She was nice and overlooked it, but I could tell—she had enough!

No one walked out during the service. Eventually people did the right thing and left the church. There are churches that should be abandoned. People stay in an awful church because of family and friends. Some stay because of relatives buried there. Many enjoy the social club and delight in running off those who don't fit in. Some people stay because they like the music. If people attempt to resolve serious issues, they are usually told to leave. We have strength in numbers; if we do what is right. Most don't have the courage to try.

Anger escalated in the evangelist. He didn't make much money. Signs, wonders, miracles, and healings didn't happen. Perhaps he sensed people didn't accept his behavior. Some display anger, when they fear being exposed. They try diverting attention; it doesn't always work. Sometimes they expose themselves.

Karen and her friend, the spiritual lady, were lying beside each other on the floor. The preacher lost his anger as he acknowledged them. He described how both had pure hearts and he spoke of how great those two women were.

Suddenly, the evangelist attacked me. He yelled, "Tony, you need to change! Tony, your wife wants you to change!" He got loud and mean. The spiritual lady lying beside my wife, laughed out loud. He called her name and said she wanted me to change. Then much louder, he asked me a question, "Tony do you know what change means?" With a louder voice I replied, "Change means different, ha-ha." People looked at me so sadly. They knew I was deeply hurt, and I was! I sat there, overwhelmed with shame and sadness. The preachers acted as if they wanted a fight. I saw the conflict emerging and wanted no part of it. I realized, I couldn't endure the foolishness. There would be another church, or I could live without one.

Suddenly, I realized how the handyman felt when he was told to leave. After he and his family completed the remodeling projects, they were run off. There were two clear choices; bow to those preachers and totally submit, or quit. Actually, I wouldn't accept the first option. I would not tolerate any more control. Why do we follow people who hate us and are headed toward the unpardonable sin?

I made up my mind at that moment, no human would ever control me. God doesn't control anyone; no person has the right. He gently encourages us to do right, but doesn't hurt or control us. "...the Lord is good; for His mercy endureth forever..." (Jer. 33:11) This is written many times throughout the Old Testament and over thirty times in Psalms.

The evangelist told another man, he needed to change. The man was humble and asked, "What has God shown you that I need to change?" The preacher rudely responded, "God will show you." The evangelist realized he was way out of line. He said in a low tone, that he needed to change. I was tempted to say amen, but kept my mouth shut. The last thing our church needed was more rudeness. Perhaps the intense sadness overwhelmed me because, I would have to leave the church. Others would be hurt, especially Karen. Sometimes, we have to make difficult choices. I loved my wife—her religion was a different story. It's no surprise—people won't attend church.

I wasn't at the next service, because I renounced that church. The pastor didn't deserve a formal resignation. My absence was enough. Others informed me what happened. They were unhappy because the evangelist mistreated people. They complained that he was especially mean to my family and me. The pastor fully supported his friend. He had excuses for his actions. The main one was, the evangelist was tired! He said his friend admitted that he got in the flesh—because he was tired. He got into more than his flesh.

Some preachers believe God will be more lenient with them because of who they are. They think He will tolerate or overlook more from them, because of their greatness. Some believe they do exceptional things, when in reality it's the opposite. Some esteem themselves greater or better than others. Preachers who think like that, will be shocked at judgment day.

God doesn't respect one person above another, and doesn't want us to show favoritism. "I charge thee before God, and the Lord Jesus Christ, and the elect angels, that thou observe these things without preferring one before another doing nothing by partiality." (1 Tim. 5:21) This means God loves us the same and will judge everyone properly. The no respecter of persons scriptures are in reference to Him judging people. You can find this in Acts 10:34. "Then Peter opened his mouth, and said, Of a truth I perceive that God is no respecter of persons:" Observe this. "To have respect of persons is not good:" This is the first part of Prov. 28:21 "For there is no respect of persons with God." (Romans 2:11) "And, ye masters, do the same things unto them, forbearing threatening: knowing that your Master also is in heaven; neither is there respect of persons with Him." (Eph. 6:9)

Why do pastors show favoritism or partiality? The word insecurity comes to my mind. They are afraid the congregation will vote them out. The larger they can build their fan club, the more votes and security they have. If a pastor stopped the control, threats and of course favoritism—they wouldn't be voted out. They wouldn't run off those who don't totally submit. I think preachers should work on their doctrines instead of a fan club.

We who teach and preach will be held to a higher standard. To whom much is known, much is required. There won't be special treatment for us. We won't be allowed to get away with any sins. We know better. The Bible definitely applies to everyone. We all need to repent, or we will perish. If certain preachers really want more glory, they need to follow Jesus; He shares the right kind.

A former pastor made this statement many years ago. He said if evil isn't stopped, it gets progressively worse. I highly respect him and I'll bet he would agree with me on this: Judgment should begin at the house of God. Peter wrote about this. If the church would get on the right path, evil wouldn't get out of control. Actually it's the Bible being fulfilled. Things will get worse, before they get better. Jesus will straighten out everything when He returns. *Even so Lord, come quickly!*

We are in the falling away period the Bible warns about. I don't expect a world-wide revival. Evil has become too widespread. We should heed the many cautions in the Bible. They warn of what happens to people who fall away, turn back or draw back unto perdition.

CHAPTER ELEVEN

THE SLOW DEATH OF A CHURCH

The pastor couldn't resolve problems in his church because he was in denial. If he had considered advise from elders, he could have saved the church. The longer he supported the evangelist, the harder it was for him to admit his mistakes. The man not only allowed the nonsense, but instigated the control.

Karen was upset because I quit. She wouldn't agree that we had serious problems, or anything might be fake. She thought wonderful healings took place. Sometimes we see what we want to, whether it's reality or not. The line between reality and faith can become blurred. Misguided faith leads people into an unseen realm of demons.

People who aren't Christians are healed, without praying or asking. Positive thinking heals people. (Prov. 23:7) "...for as he thinketh in his heart, so is he..." God designed healing to naturally take place. Why do we have ridiculous shows, get prideful, and exalt ourselves?

Some pick and choose from God's Word. We should believe it all, or we could be in serious trouble. If we don't believe it all, we're taking away from it. We can't take words out of the Bible, but we can take away—from them. Many misinterpret much of the Bible.

God Shall Take Away His Part
Out Of The Book Of Life

"For I testify unto every man that heareth the words of the prophecy of this book, If any man shall add unto these things, God shall add unto him the plagues that are written in this book: And if any man shall take away from the words of the book of this prophecy, God shall take away his part out of the book of life, and out of the holy city, and from the things which are written in this book." (Rev. 22:18–19)

Look how Moses tried to negotiate with God. "Yet now, if thou wilt forgive their sin; and if not, blot me, I pray thee, out of thy book which thou hast written. And the Lord said unto Moses, Whosoever hath sinned against me, him will I blot out of my book." (Ex. 32:32–33) Jesus Christ declared this, "He that overcometh, the same shall be clothed in white raiment; and I will not blot out his name out of the book of life, but I will confess his name before my Father, and before his angels." (Rev. 3:5)

We overcome through faith in Jesus Christ. He won't blot our name out of the book of life if we follow Him, overcome and stop taking away from His Word. Jesus made it plain, we won't perish or lose our salvation if we follow and obey Him. I'm interpreting John 10:27–28. In John chapter fifteen, Jesus makes it crystal clear; we must bear fruit. Bearing fruit is doing good things. (works)

It's wrong to add to the words in the Bible and have a plague come upon us. It's worse to take away from the words, and miss heaven. Hell will have many residents who were good—religious people. They think cautions in the Bible don't apply to them. His Word applies to everyone and most cautions in the New Testament were addressed to Christians!

Some say speaking in tongues is of the devil; tongues have ceased, and there is no baptism of the Holy Ghost. Would you declare this; there is no baptism of the Holy Spirit? Most agree; the Holy Spirit and Holy Ghost are the same. We shouldn't deny either baptism; both are in His Word. I love all the baptisms or experiences in Jesus Christ; they are wonderful.

I wrote earlier, God's Spirits are like the same; let me elaborate. They are alike, but have different functions. Jesus refers to the Spirit of truth three times in John. In one verse He refers to the Spirit of truth as another Comforter. Jesus said He would be in us. The Comforter, Spirit of Truth, and the Holy Spirit are in us if we're saved and so is Jesus!

Some think the trinity, (Father, Son and Holy Spirit) is a mystery. The Spirits of God are far beyond three. Revelation mentions seven Spirits of God. (Rev. 3:1) More than seven are found in His Word. No one fully understands God; He is complex. God is three entities that are like the same and His attributes are far-reaching.

Some believe baptism is emersion in water, a cleansing, purification and symbolism. It is that and more. A baptism is an experience. It's anything we're introduced to, or an initiation to something. It could be biblical or secular. All biblical baptisms are contained within the main one. How else could the Bible proclaim there is one baptism and also mention six or more? Don't deny any baptism or anything else in the Bible!

Remember the baptism of Moses and John. There is the baptism into Jesus Christ. (main one) There is a baptism of repentance, water, by fire, into His death, Holy Spirit and Holy Ghost. Some deny many biblical baptisms. I don't know which baptisms, if any, you could deny and still have salvation. I'm not going to reject any part of Jesus. To resist, reject or deny the baptism, or introduction to the Holy Spirit or Holy Ghost could be blasphemy. This is the sin God will not forgive.

Here are more false teachings. We should fall to the floor when someone lays hands on us and prays. This is not written in the Bible. Someone should catch people when they fall under the power of God. That isn't in His Word. Do you think these false teachings could be traditions of men? You got it! We shouldn't lean to our understanding; lean on His Word. Most everyone knows He is the final authority and so is His Word. Wrong traditions can easily lead us to the place of torment and pain. Don't follow a false prophet to hell.

How could God allow our free will if He is always in control? He allows us to reap what we sow, The bad, good—and the ugly. He allows foolish things and accidents. That isn't control and He hopes we'll learn from our mistakes. He loves us and always will.

God allows us to choose heaven or hell. If He was always in control, He would control us into heaven. Did God control Hitler or allow him to have those evil thoughts? Did He cause him to kill several million of His own chosen people? (Jews) Do you think God caused millions to die in World War II? God allows sin, but He doesn't tempt or want us to sin. We control that.

I've misinterpreted the Bible in the past, because of false teachings. Some think, God won't hold us accountable, because we were taught wrong. God said, "I will put my laws into their hearts and in their minds will I write them." (last part of Heb. 10:16) We are without excuse.

If a fire kills two of three children a couple has, would that be God's will? If the parents abused and killed their remaining child, how could we say that was God's will? Some would say God did it because He doesn't make mistakes. It's true He doesn't make mistakes but that doesn't mean He does awful things to us. If God controlled everything, He sure has caused horrible atrocities in this world. He lets us make the mess! He allows bad things through our free will, so we'll learn from our mistakes and realize how much we need His help.

One thing He can't be blamed for is our ignorance. The Bible makes it plain—God is not willing that anyone should perish. I'm paraphrasing 2 Peter 3:9. He allows us to perish. Sometimes God lets our will prevail over His. He loves us so much; He lets us do what we want. That my friend is not control; it's love!

(Heb. 9:27) "And as it is appointed unto men once to die, but after this the judgment:" The Bible doesn't say, we have an appointed time to die. "For the wages of sin is death; but the gift of God is eternal life through Jesus Christ our Lord." (Rom. 6:23) We have all sinned; we all must die. Therefore it is appointed unto men—once to die. Some misquote and misinterpret that verse by saying this: We have an appointed time to die. They immediately contradict by saying, but you can rush it.

Do you see why my wife Karen, along with others, would leave churches? The full gospel churches teach more of, "every word that proceedeth out of the mouth of God" like Jesus said. They teach with more accuracy than most, but sometimes add things they shouldn't.

Those who take away from God's Word in a big way, will have their names blotted out of His book. If our name is removed from the book of life, we shall not enter heaven. "And whosoever was not found written in the book of life was cast into the lake of fire." (Rev. 20:15) If it's blotted out, taken out or erased, it's all the same; we miss heaven. Some believe this; God doesn't have an eraser. God has many types of erasers. He created all things and owns everything. The comment was made in reference to a popular false doctrine. "I, even I, am he that blotteth out thy transgressions for mine own sake, and will not remember thy sins." (Isaiah 43:25) "And their sins and iniquities will I remember no more." (Heb. 10:17) The blood of Jesus Christ erases sin.

People that take away from the words of the Bible, and don't overcome things, will have their names erased from the book of life. We should do our best to not misinterpret God's Word. How else do you think we could—take away from the words?

The Bible declares, "...For unto whomsoever much is given, of him shall be much required..." (Luke 12:48) He forgives sin we commit in ignorance. Jesus is God and He knows how to pray effectively to His Father. He prayed this prayer for us, "Father, forgive them; for they know not what they do." (Luke 23:34) I'm sure God answered that prayer. However, He has given us so much, He requires much.

I told Karen, her church would dissolve if her pastor wouldn't change. She thought we would divorce if she didn't leave the church. I said, "How are you going to feel if you lose me and your church? How could you give up your husband for a church that is destined to close?" I explained, " I don't want you to abandon the church. I appreciate anyone who is loyal to their convictions and doesn't give up on their beliefs. I want you to hang in there until you're struggling to pay the rent." It took a year to dissolve. If leaders won't change, they should be removed. Sometimes, members quit and leaders have to leave. Members should—cut the money off!

Karen wanted me to return. I tried convincing her there were fake falls, signs, wonders and false prophets. We had intense discussions but she believed in the church as strongly as I believed my convictions. It was always a stalemate.

She got upset when I explained how things were set up and staged. I demonstrated fake falls in our home. Karen became angry when I spoke against what she adored. She stated, her falls were from God and she couldn't be brainwashed. When we are controlled and brainwashed, we don't realize it. If you were a victim of this, you would be devastated. It can break your heart, literally as in Karen's case. A massive heart attack killed Karen instantly. I can't go back and re-live my life. I can help people recognize similar problems in their lives. With God's help, they can avoid pain, suffering, loss of money, time, and above all, loss of life. If you're in a similar situation, get help.

I reminded Karen of the week we spent at summer camp with boys and girls from our church. The pastor in charge of the event had impressive credentials. He made a profound statement. "There will be a morning and evening service every day this week. There will be people praying for others. I don't want to see anyone falling to make someone look good. By the same token, I don't want someone resisting the power of God." Karen didn't realize that people fake falls.

Wonderful things happened that week. Many accepted Jesus as their Lord and Savior. I didn't see anyone fall. When things are decent and in order, good things happen. "Let all things be done decently and in order." (1 Cor. 14:40) I said, "Karen, think about what the man said; surely he has seen people faking falls to look spiritual. Don't we want to receive from God? Isn't it possible we try too hard and fall under the power of suggestions or trickery?"

It was time for my Gauley trip to West Virginia. Summersville Lake is lowered in the fall, for flood control. Below the dam, the release of water creates fun for whitewater enthusiasts like my friends and me.

Every year we raft this world-class river. People from all over the world enjoy this whitewater, rated in the top ten in the world. It contains an intense display of powerful rapids. The river deserves respect and requires a guide, unless you're an expert! Please study maps, stay with a group and follow someone.

As the guide and supplier of gear and equipment, I'm responsible for the success or failure of a river trip. For over forty years, I've been fortunate to keep us safe on whitewater rivers. I give my guide Jesus Christ, all the credit. I couldn't navigate this river without His help.

Karen was upset because I was going to West Virginia. She said I should be in church instead. She asked, "What river are you going to?" I replied, "It's time for the famous fall Gauley." There was a look of terror on her face. She asked, "Isn't it rated in the top ten most dangerous rivers?" I said, "No Sweetie, the Gauley River is rated in the top ten most popular rivers in the world." She asked, "Aren't the popular rivers the most dangerous?" I said, "Well, sort of, but not exactly. There are many rivers in the world more dangerous than the Gauley." I said, "We've rafted the Gauley for years without any problems." She exclaimed in fear, "But honey, we don't have insurance; what if you get crippled or killed?" She didn't act like this before; it puzzled me.

I assumed Karen wasn't worried about me; she was trying to get me back in church. I would rather be destroyed by the river, than false prophets. I told Karen, "I don't live my life in fear; I prepare for our safety on river trips. You can't use fear to scare me back to the church."

Karen looked surprised and apologized. She said, "I'm sorry honey, I know you're always careful on a river. I just want you back in church." I asked if she would let me choose our next church when that one closed. She replied "No!" It was the answer I expected. Karen was determined to have her style of a full gospel church.

The river trip to West Virginia came and went as they do every year: no problems, no worries. As usual, Karen wasn't excited to see me. She didn't worry about us, or did she? In hindsight, perhaps there was something going on with her, that I was unaware of. Maybe she was more upset than I realized. The wrong crowd caused extensive damage. Karen rarely showed emotion, especially the negative kind. Her faith ignored problems to a fault. Perhaps she worried about many things, especially in her church. Stress overwhelmed—and caused her demise.

I didn't realize this until after Karen's death. Sometimes a person's faith causes denial of serious problems. Something terrible was going on in Karen's body. It was like a bomb waiting to explode. She didn't suspect serious problems. Later, tests showed the possibility of bleeding ulcers.

Deep inside, Karen knew I was right about the church. A friend of hers informed me of this after Karen died. The church was beginning to die and so was Karen. I didn't know she was stressed to that extent; her faith had it hidden. Had I known, I would have taken any measures to help her.

Sometimes people think God and church are synonymous. They are not the same. Often, a church receives so much attention, people are neglected. When anyone neglects their spouse because of a church, priorities are out of order. Some churches should be forsaken.

The pastor's wife called, about nine months after I quit. She told me God impressed her to call, to tell me how much she loved me. I told the woman I loved them. She said I would be very successful and blessed.

A week later, her husband called. He introduced himself without using his title of pastor. His humility was refreshing and he wanted to apologize to my family and me. He said since the incident took place at church, that was where the apology should be made. I asked him what was his apology for. Of course, I had a good idea; I wanted to hear him say it. Do you remember the expression; confession is good for the soul?

He explained, he was going to apologize for the evangelist being too mean. Immediately, he took away the apology by making the excuse, he was tired. I thought oh no, here we go again!

I asked, "Why did it take God nine months to tell you mistakes were made?" His lame excuse was, he was confused. I'm sure he was, and the devil had him where he wants everyone. I've been there. I explained, "When a mean sermon is preached, it's delivered to everyone. The apology should be to everyone." I asked if he wanted to call the others that left, or should I call them? He said, "Tony, you could probably do a better job talking to them than I could." I told the preacher I would think about his offer and call him later.

The preacher wasn't going to apologize for his part. He wanted me to help restore his church, without admitting any wrong doing on his part or his friend. He wouldn't relinquish his control or express remorse.

A few days later, I called the young man. I told him if I thought he could give a sincere apology whereby he could save his church, I would help. Gently, I explained why it wouldn't work. I tried convincing the preacher what was wrong. He wouldn't admit to control, fake things, or extortion. I dealt with his problems to no avail. I hoped he had changed but I didn't see any evidence. Sadly, after several days and many talks, I gave up. The church closed a few months later.

We haven't seen persecution like the saints of old; it doesn't mean our time isn't near. We live in perilous times; be ready. Jesus spoke about His return. (second coming) Most believe it's near.

"And then shall appear the sign of the Son of man in heaven: and then shall all the tribes of the earth mourn, and they shall see the Son of man coming in the clouds of heaven with power and great glory. And he shall send his angels with a great sound of a trumpet, and they shall gather together his elect from the four winds, from one end of heaven to the other." (Mt. 24:30–31) "For the Lord himself shall descend from heaven with a shout, with the voice of the archangel, and with the trump of God: and the dead in Christ shall rise first: Then we which are alive and remain shall be caught up together with them in the clouds, to meet the Lord in the air: and so shall we ever be with the Lord." (1 Th. 4:16–17) We call this the rapture of the church, the elect or saved.

I'm ready to meet Jesus in the air and go to my new home. It's our choice; please choose life. We have only two choices, heaven or hell. Some believe other ways lead to eternal life; that is false. There is one way; I'm positive because many scriptures explain this. People believe what they want, but that doesn't make it true. At times we are unsure of the truth. Don't doubt what Jesus said.

Jesus Christ said truly, truly or "Verily, verily I say unto you, He that entereth not by the door into the sheepfold, but climbeth up some other way, the same is a thief and a robber." (John 10:1) We find in John 10:7, "Then said Jesus unto them again, Verily, verily I say unto you, I am the door of the sheep." Why do some believe another way leads to heaven? Perhaps they believe following Jesus is too difficult and they don't want to obey a King.

If someone was in a foreign country ruled by a king, they would probably bow to him. If the king told them to do something, they would do it out of respect or fear, maybe both. Please accept Jesus more than an earthly king; He expects and deserves it.

Jesus Christ left heaven, became a human and suffered horribly. He desires that all mankind accept His free gift of salvation. Stop religion and idol worship. If you don't, you'll live to regret it forever! The devil and his demons don't want us to believe in God. Some believe this; God, the devil, heaven and hell are fairy tales and don't exist. Think of the people who were eyewitnesses of Jesus Christ. We know many wrote about these things. The sacred writings were passed from one generation to the next. Men of God diligently prayed over what writings should be called God's Word. I've seen enough evidence to believe in God as Creator, Savior and supplier of all our needs!

Walk outside and take a good long look. We should be able to recognize and accept Him by our faith; we can't please Him without it! Some don't realize faith is an essential part of our salvation. We are saved by grace through faith. True saving faith has action, works and fruit. God's Word explains faith has substance and evidence.

The King of kings is here now in Spirit. He wants a little closer—inside your heart. He says, behold, I stand at the door and knock. Open your heart, be willing to change, obey, follow Jesus Christ and He will come in. You can fellowship with the Creator of everything and inherit everything in the universe. "He that overcometh shall inherit all things; and I will be his God and he shall be my son." (Rev. 21:7) His way is hard at times, but easier than living without Him. He loves us so much; He died for all, so we might live forever.

CHAPTER TWELVE

KAREN'S FINAL MONTHS BEFORE DEATH

I suspected Karen was upset because the church was reduced to almost nothing. She didn't tell me it had closed. A woman revealed to me what my wife couldn't.

Karen told me she was hurting. I didn't feel like the one who could console her. It's horrible when a husband and wife aren't spiritually compatible. A couple should be compatible in other things as well. Spiritual matters should be the main area where they agree. Instead she turned to her friend, the spiritual lady.

They called the evangelist who lived a hundred miles from us. He preached several times for our former church. Someone who had special gifts and miracles, was who they wanted. The preacher took their offer, drove to Taylorsville once a week and taught the Bible study. Karen purchased an ad in our local newspaper and rented a commercial building. She wrote, if you need a miracle, come to the Bible study.

We find special gifts in First Corinthians chapter twelve. Look at verses seven through ten. "But the manifestation of the Spirit is given to every man to profit withal. For to one is given by the Spirit the word of wisdom; to another the word of knowledge by the same Spirit; To another faith by the same Spirit; to another the gifts of healing by the same Spirit; To another the working of miracles; to another prophecy; to another discerning of spirits; to another divers kinds of tongues; to another the interpretation of tongues."

If anyone wants evidence where God did miracles through people, look in Acts 6:8, 8:6, and 19:11. These are just a few; there are many more. Spirits of devils can work miracles. (Rev. 16:14) False prophets are allowed to do miracles. (Rev. 19:20)

The spiritual women wasted no time and rented a place. The false prophet was ready to teach. While lacking enthusiasm, I didn't show it. Karen had high expectations for the endeavor because the man really put on a show. I couldn't get interested; something didn't seem right. The Holy Spirit was warning me.

Several women and I attended the first Bible study. I didn't go back. I felt like the preacher was wrong in too many areas. I had enough of the religion Karen loved so dearly. After twenty years of following her religion, I couldn't accept it. My marriage was different; I loved Karen and hoped some day we would find what was missing in our lives.

Karen was angry, because I wouldn't support the Bible study she hoped would grow into a church. I explained to her, that by allowing her to pay rent on the building and the preacher, I was indeed supporting her Bible study. Of course, Karen wanted me at the meetings. I couldn't take it anymore.

She asked if the preacher teaching the Bible study could be a false prophet. I told her I wasn't sure, but I suspected it. God will judge who is and isn't. When Jesus was speaking about false prophets in Matthew chapter seven, He explained how we would know them. He implied, we would know everyone by their fruits. "Beware of false prophets, which come to you in sheep's clothing, but inwardly they are ravening wolves. Ye shall know them by their fruits. Do men gather grapes of thorns, or figs of thistles? Even so every good tree bringeth forth good fruit; but a corrupt tree bringeth forth evil fruit. A good tree cannot bring forth evil fruit, neither can a corrupt tree bring forth good fruit. Every tree that bringeth not forth good fruit is hewn down, and cast into the fire. Wherefore by their fruits ye shall know them." (Mt. 7:15–20)

Their actions will give the insight we need, to determine what they are. When I told Karen I strongly suspected the evangelist was a false prophet, I didn't say he was. I didn't know for sure; but I know now by his actions and the Holy Spirit.

The Bible Says A Soft Answer Turns Away Wrath

Karen exploded with anger and threats of divorce. I showed her nothing but genuine love. The Bible says, a soft answer turns away wrath. After Karen was calm, I explained I might be wrong about the preacher. I hoped their Bible study would grow into the church that we desired for twenty years. After a sincere promise that I would do nothing to hurt the Bible study, she seemed satisfied. I said, "If this is of God, it will work; if it isn't, it won't. If everything works out, I'll join later."

Karen spent a lot of money advertising the weekly studies. I didn't complain, though we couldn't afford it. I hoped someday Karen and I would reconcile differences and live happily ever after. I didn't realize death was already working in her. Several months later as she lay in a coma, tests showed the possibility of bleeding ulcers. After three days in the hospital and many tests, there was no hope.

God Is Pouring Out His Spirit In These Last Days

Maybe the Holy Spirit revealed to others what He showed me. He must have told people to stay away from the Bible studies. The meetings lasted several months. I realize God is pouring out His Spirit in these last days. People notice false teachings and find many things disturbing. We can't always trust what some do in the name of Jesus. Be suspicious of anything that doesn't line up with His Word. It's difficult to hear the voice of God, if we don't know His Word. We all need help and some direction in our lives.

If we know His Word, we know Jesus, and the voice of a stranger we won't follow. "And a stranger they will not follow, but will flee from him:

for they know not the voice of strangers." (John 10:5) "My sheep hear my voice, and I know them, and they follow me." (John 10:27) If we follow Jesus we won't perish and no one can take eternal life from us. The next verse is that promise. "And I give unto them eternal life; and they shall never perish, neither shall any man pluck them out of my hand." (John 10:28) It is so sad; many people don't know we have to follow Him, which means obey. It makes the promise conditional.

I know two promises God made, that aren't conditional. I feel sure there are more. He promised to never leave or forsake us. How could He, God is everywhere. He made it clear; nothing shall separate us from His love. How could He stop loving; God is Love. Some believe these two promises mean, they can live like the heathen and still make it to heaven. They don't heed the cautions in His Word that were written to Christians. Some think we don't have to do anything, because salvation is not of works. It is true salvation is not derived from, or of works, but it is through our works. We are saved by grace through faith. The works of faith in Jesus Christ are necessary. Most don't consider that we are justified by faith and works; it's in the King James Bible. The works and sealed doctrines are misunderstood. We will study these important doctrines in a later chapter. This is fascinating and will amaze people how most of us—have been wrong for much of our lives.

Most are not accepting the fake and false magic show tricks, or the people who have a form of godliness, but deny the power thereof. We should turn away from those who are like that. (paraphrasing 2 Tim. 3:5) People want the whole truth, a comprehensive teaching and nothing added or—taken away. There is in fact no substitution for the great truth in God's Holy Word.

Two months before Karen's death, and the closing of the Bible study, she exploded on me again. About sixty days prior to her death, she was perhaps the meanest and cruelest she had been in twenty years of marriage. It was totally out of character; she was a kind and loving person. Karen was fading away, and I couldn't see it. *Father please help people learn from my mistakes. I ask in the name of Jesus, the name above all names.*

I misunderstood the nature of her problem; consequently I didn't respond properly. If I had been aware, maybe I could have saved her life. She was suffering with depression, stress and anxiety. She most likely feared the Bible study would close. I learned later, she realized I was right about the church.

It's possible Karen also feared—I was right about her Bible study preacher being a false prophet. Her stress accumulated over many years. Of course, I had no idea the extent of her depression or problems.

Many full gospel churches are doctrinally sound and many aren't. The problems in that religion are similar to problems in others; they don't follow their own Bibles.

Karen loved God and people so much; she wouldn't be drawn to a weird church intentionally. She was prideful; it would have been hard for her to admit she was wrong. Admitting that she wouldn't allow her husband to become the head of his wife, (biblically speaking) would also be difficult. We men must earn this right! Husbands who don't submit to God can't expect a Godly woman to submit to them.

It was my fault; I didn't earn the right. I should've studied the Bible and had my heart right. A man should be the leader in the home. He can't rule his house well if he isn't the leader. When he isn't qualified, his wife has no choice but to lead. We should lead with love and submissiveness. (paraphrasing Eph. 5:21–25) This is used to teach proper roles for a husband and wife.

Since I didn't see what was happening to Karen, I couldn't react properly. We didn't see the warning signs. This is where hindsight is important. This is where everyone must focus carefully in order to recognize when serious problems exist, and need correcting. These are matters of life and death. Learn from our mistakes and live.

Anger had been escalating in Karen. She was tired and not feeling well. I noticed this about two weeks before she passed. Unfortunately, I didn't see the connection in these events. Karen needed a doctor; she was in serious trouble and headed for a disaster. Karen was dying, and I couldn't see it. During the three days in the hospital, they discovered her hemoglobin was extremely low, due to possible internal bleeding. This explained the changes: anger, tiredness, and weight gain, especially in her abdomen. She was craving sugar and buying three times more desserts than usual.

Karen and I needed a good counselor. We had too much pride, the sinful kind. I should have stayed humble, regardless of how much God blessed and no matter how talented or gifted I was. When I exalted myself, I was humbled. It hurt more than anyone could imagine.

Karen's anger cut like a knife. I was deeply hurt but didn't show it. I didn't return evil for evil. With meekness, I told Karen she should be like Apostle Paul. He learned contentment with any situation he found himself in, and even praised God in his sufferings. I guess you could say, Tony just didn't have a clue what was happening.

I loved Karen with everything I had. She mentioned divorce again. I refused to discuss it and tried to show her nothing but pure love. For about the next two months, right up until she died, I couldn't take my eyes off her. I was very kind but realized too late, that she needed a doctor.

Our love was never more sweet or intense in many years. A few weeks before Karen died, she admitted how much she loved me. I was thankful for this closeness, for a two-month period before she left. God blessed me with her special love, before she went home to heaven. It's a great comfort, knowing she had her heart right with God.

One day Karen said, "The Bible study has been shut down." There was no emotion in her voice. She was subdued and withdrawn. I didn't know what to say; I remained silent. Karen drifted into another world. Finally, she admitted that she didn't feel well. I was at a loss for words.

The false prophet left town. My Karen had a heart attack four days later and died instantly in my arms. Karen shouted "Tony" and fell to the bathroom floor. After lifting her to a sitting position attempting to revive her, I knew Karen wasn't breathing and didn't have a pulse. I ran out the front door pressing 911 on my phone. My resuscitator was in the garage and Karen needed it.

After telling the lady at communications what happened, I went to work with perfect CPR. The experts arrived shortly, and asked me to continue while they set up their equipment. They knew us; in fact their leader was a friend of ours. He struggled trying to hide his emotions; I knew by his expression, Karen was in a terrible state. The EMTs, paramedics, and I brought her back after forty minutes. She didn't regain consciousness, but at least she had a pulse. CPR must produce a pulse within a few minutes or brain damage begins to occur. The hospital did their best, for three days. The doctors ran many tests. Eventually, we had to concede the inevitable and let her go.

Someone told me at Iredell Memorial Hospital, the ambulance crew got a pulse as they entered the parking lot. I had high hopes for her recovery. I felt a slight pain in my left wrist for a year, after being so aggressive trying to save Karen. Spraining my wrist was nothing to me; I would have done anything to save her. I knew Karen died, but after we got a pulse, I thought we brought her back and saved her life.

Three days later, one of Karen's doctors tried his best to comfort me before he said, "I have to recommend—we turn off life support." He said, "Don't beat yourself up son, I read the paramedic's report. Even with perfect CPR, if you don't get a pulse within four minutes, the brain begins to die. Over the past three days, her brain activity has steadily declined and we must give up." I asked, "Isn't there anything you can do?" Almost in tears, two doctors moved their heads side to side as they choked up and said, "no." I entered another world of sadness and shock.

Karen received the best of care at Iredell Memorial in Statesville, North Carolina. Her family and I felt like she was given extra special treatment. Nurses talked long after Karen died, about feeling something different in her room and on the whole floor. They felt God's Presence. Perhaps there were angels reassuring people that it was okay. I believe her spirit left her body the moment of the heart attack, and where she went, no one would want to come back. Karen Little was with wonderful people, angels and best of all, her Lord and Savior—Jesus Christ.

I believe with every fiber within my being, she is in heaven. I don't say this just because I want to believe it. After twenty years of marriage, certainly I knew her better than anyone, except for God. He absolutely knows what is in our heart. Karen Little had her heart right!

CHAPTER THIRTEEN

SATAN TRIES TO KILL ME

T hank God for Karen's children. I don't view them as step children. I view them as precious, and love them as my own. They may have saved my life. In times like these, you discover who knows how to love. Their support came at the most difficult time of my life.

Some people aren't supportive during a time like this. Some saw an opportunity to finish me off. They assumed I was in a weakened state and it would be easy to destroy me. Many attempts have been made, none successful. God is my refuge and strength.

The attacks began a few weeks after Karen died. I wasn't sleeping well, had no appetite, and eating was difficult. My emotions were in turmoil. I hadn't been to church in a long time; I was physically, and spiritually the weakest I had ever been. I was heading for a disaster! My mind wasn't functioning properly. I felt as if a part of me had been ripped out and thrown away. It was an opportune time for demons to annihilate me. Since they are spirit beings, it's wise to consider their methods of attack. If we understand our enemy, we have a defense.

Evil spirits want people to follow wicked ideas and do things that cause our demise. They'll steal everything, especially our peace and faith. Demons influence us to sin, if we aren't following God's Word. Prayer and reading the Bible isn't enough. James wrote, "But be ye doers of the word, and not hearers only, deceiving your own selves." (James 1:22) Wrong thoughts come, think on good things and demons leave.

Jesus explained, we should listen to Him and not the other voices. Our thoughts are sometimes—demons. If we don't know how to listen, who to listen to, and how to think, we'll get into trouble. I've been there most of my life. It's imperative we think right, speak right and do right.

Bold statements inform demons, causing them to relay messages to the devil. He sends more evil spirits to kill us. If we make bold remarks, we should be secure in our relationship with God. What I said to initiate these horrendous attacks was this: "I will do great things for God and lead thousands of people to Jesus and heaven."

I can't save anyone, but I can lead people to the one who can. Lost people think they can party and sin, until they decide to accept Jesus. They hope to slide in at the last minute. There is a good probability it won't happen. Don't think you can enjoy sin all your life and get His salvation whenever you want.

The Bible says, "...behold, now is the accepted time; behold, now is the day of salvation." (2 Cor. 6:2) Sometimes we are stubborn and want everything our way. To let anyone rule us as king or lord is out of the realm of possibility; we think. Think again. No submission means no salvation. No works of faith means not bearing fruit. We should know where we'll end up if we don't bear fruit.

We aren't promised tomorrow. God's promises of long life are conditional. They work if we meet conditions His Word describes. He knows through free will, we can have a fatal accident. There are things God insists, having His way. (John 6:44) "No man can come to Me, except the Father which hath sent Me draw him..." If you think God has quit drawing, it may be too late, but don't give up; we can't make that call. Only God can judge that. Most people don't know, when God gives up on someone, it's impossible for them to have salvation. Jesus made it plain; we have to be drawn by His Father. God knows what we'll decide. He knows if we will accept Jesus or not. He strives with someone to gather evidence He wants for His courtroom. At judgment day, He may remind people of the times He knocked on their heart's door.

If you feel Him drawing right now, accept His free gift. The Creator dwelling inside us is better than any sins demons could bring our way. Don't believe it's too late; only God knows that. Now is the day for salvation, right now. Now is the accepted time, not later!

Before I discuss the satanic attacks, I must explain they were coming through a lot of people. Thank God, Karen and I had many friends, or the attacks could have been overwhelming. The devil and his demons use anyone they can to hurt us. God gave us the power to overcome demonic forces. (His Spirit)

If thoughts don't line up with God's Word, give us peace and faith, they aren't from God. Don't listen to the voice of another; you could get hurt or killed. Sometimes, we forget sin causes death. "For the wages of sin is death..." (Rom. 6:23) There are sins that kill quickly and others are a slow torture, we can't seem to detect. The essence of deception is—we don't realize it's happening. I've been there most of my life because I didn't study. I'm thankful He didn't give up on me. God is good and His mercy endures forever; that doesn't mean we can wait forever!

Friends and family can hurt or kill. Pray for them, even if they act like enemies. We'll have attacks once we take a stand for God; however, we win if we stay close to Him. I could ignore most of the attacks.

One episode was unbelievable, requiring my undivided attention; it almost killed me. Miracles happen all the time. There is no doubt, I received a miracle. I love my Father in heaven; He delivers us from evil.

Soon after Karen's death, I sold my home. I felt this would stop the awful nightmares; it worked. I made a business transaction with a woman. When someone learned of this, they criticized me for doing business with her. They thought if I wasn't careful, people would think I killed my wife because of this woman.

I barely knew her. My business deal was, in my opinion, a small insignificant thing. I tried ignoring the nonsense, but it bothered me. It was only a few weeks after Karen died and I was in a weakened state. My accuser thought I was acting strange. It's true; I was frustrated and overwhelmed with grief. We act different when an event devastates us.

The false accusation really bothered me. I forgot to eat the rest of that day or night. Sleep was almost nonexistent, while I tossed and turned all night. I got up before daylight to go for a drive.

Sunrise found me on a road in the western part of our county called Devil Track. Stressed beyond the point of overload, I fainted while traveling about fifty miles per hour. My car drifted off the road, hit a fence and a tree. The tree stopped my car abruptly; it almost overturned. The airbag provided a huge favor and woke me. My head needed a jolt and the airbag was the solution. Except for slight numbness in my face, I felt perfectly normal—that was strange after feeling sick earlier.

There was smoke inside the car and my front doors were jammed. I crawled into the back seat and exited one of the rear doors. Two men ran out of their homes to check on their fence and tree. They didn't seem concerned about me. Walking to the men, I asked, "Do I have any facial injuries?" The first one said, "You look bad." The second man said, "You look fine to me." I accepted the second man's remark.

Thank God, no one was hurt. The Lord prevented me from any injury whatsoever. Sometimes we forget how helpless we are. Thank God for His angels and protection. Before the day was over, the same person harassed me again. The person said people would think I was having an affair with the business lady, killed her husband and his friend, before I killed Karen. Can we say—an imagination running wild?

Some thought it was a laughing matter, because the lies were so outlandish. Who would murder three people, because they were having an adulterous affair? Repulsive lies like that could literally destroy someone. It wasn't amusing to me; it was absolutely ridiculous.

Thankfully no one believed the lies. Maybe people didn't believe the person, because of a troubled past with alcohol and drugs. I love this person and forgive them.

I informed the business lady of the ugly lies. I didn't want her to hear it from someone else. Oddly, this caused us to become friends. The friendship was short because of gossip, and it upset her. She decided we couldn't be friends and I agreed. People would never stop gossiping. For their benefit, we decided to end the friendship. I didn't conduct any more business with her and we didn't have an affair.

The person who started this, decided to tell the Alexander County Sheriff's Department. I heard about it indirectly. The cops didn't contact me or investigate the ridiculous story, but I did contact them.

I explained it to the sheriff like this: "I'm willing to answer any questions from anyone, while waiving my Miranda rights and I will do so without an attorney present." The sheriff told me the same thing his detective said, "Tony, you are not under investigation." He said there wasn't any evidence against me, and unless someone produced evidence, there would be no investigation. The sheriff told me I could take care of this problem and that I should. He declared, "You do have a serious problem, but you can handle it."

I spoke to everyone who had discussed the sick rumor. They told me the same thing, "The person telling those lies must be crazy." I knew rumors could spread in this small town. Would anyone want me in their home cleaning floors or carpets if they heard those hideous lies? For that matter, who would want me in their church, business or office?

How could anyone think I was capable of killing three people in order to have a secret lover? It sounded like something in the movies. The lies were imagined, or planted by demons to destroy me. It certainly would have hurt to see my carpet cleaning business destroyed. Had it not been for divine protection, I could have been killed.

The sheriff gave good advice, "You fix the problem Tony." Most people said to forget about it. I decided proactive was the best approach. I wrote a thank you letter to the public. Our local newspaper was the best way to deliver the message. I've been blessed with friends, and wanted to thank them. No one believed the false accusations of a sex scandal and triple homicide—because there was no evidence. Thank God no one tried to manufacture evidence! When there is no evidence of something, it doesn't exist. Notice I didn't say, if you can't find any evidence. I said if there is no evidence. Soon afterwards, I heard of a forensic lab in North Carolina, falsifying some of their reports. The lab helped convict innocent people and send them to death row. Some people do anything for fame and fortune. Thank God they were caught. Telling lies, to put someone on death row is horrible. Believe me, I know exactly how it feels being the recipient of that evil.

At the end of the thank you letter to the public, I asked readers to look at next week's edition of The Taylorsville Times for a second letter. I explained the letter could save women's lives.

The second letter had a hidden agenda. I wanted a simple disclosure of Karen's death, without anyone knowing what I was attempting. I gave precise events, phone calls, and every piece of evidence I could think of, to explain what happened. Some viewed the second letter as strange. If the rumors had spread, the letter could protect me from the onslaught that could destroy my reputation. I was fighting for my life. Thank God no one believed the lies. They were too irrational.

I believe the second letter should be reprinted. Remember, I was grieving and my emotions were in turmoil. It doesn't surprise me some thought the letter was strange. It was an attempt to disclose the ordeal and maybe protect me.

LETTER TO THE PUBLIC
By Tony Little

This is a continuance from my letter of last week explaining how women could possibly avoid a deadly heart attack.

Karen Little was 53 years old, seemingly in good health, a hard worker, and she looked about 40. She started having some low level chest pain about 24 hours before she died. At her request, I purchased medicine for heartburn, indigestion and gas. Nothing seemed to help her.

About two hours before she died, I said, "I bet you wish you had gone to the doctor today." She answered not a word and gave me a sad look. I replied, "If you aren't any better in the morning, I'm going to take you to the doctor." We were both very reluctant to ever go to a doctor. I think it was around nine o'clock when Mila called her. They had a nice long conversation. Mila recalled later, "She seemed tired." After she hung up the phone, she went to the bathroom. As soon as she opened the toothpaste, she shouted, "Tony!" and hit the floor.

I arrived on the scene in three seconds. My assessment of her condition took less than ten seconds. After calling 911, I ran to the garage to retrieve a resuscitator, and began CPR. The EMTs arrived soon afterward and did an outstanding job. Karen remained with no pulse for about 40 minutes. I believe it was a miracle they got one at all.

Three days later, we had to make an informed decision. It was hard, but we let her go. I saw her die once; I did not want to see her die again. Ladies and gentlemen, listen up. Do not take my word for this, but seek expert advice. I've been hearing from a lot of people that women do not experience heart attack symptoms as severe as men do. If this is true, a person could easily misdiagnose a possible heart attack. It seems to me that if you get no relief soon after you try some medicine: GO TO THE DOCTOR.

Some say heart attacks and strokes are the number one killers of women in this country. Are we men shifting stress or workload or both onto our wives? I believe I did, without realizing what I was doing. I should have helped her more around the house. I should have helped her pay the bills. I should have helped her more with the grandchildren. I should have walked a closer walk with God. All through the years, I thought I did. I can see with crystal clear persuasion that I did not. If I had indeed walked a closer walk with God, Karen would not have asked me several times in our twenty-year marriage for marriage counseling. Of course, Mr. Know-It-All refused. It is quite possible we both ignored serious differences, and just loved each other anyway. Maybe I ignored them, and she let them stress her to death.

I wish churches all over this county would hand pick a few men and women full of the Holy Ghost and wisdom to be special counselors. I wish the pastor would always mention after every service that special counselors are available right now to talk to you about anything you need to talk about, in private in a back room.

There are many scriptures that show us God wants us to live a long life. Since we are to live by every word that proceeds out of the mouth of God, we certainly have to compare scriptures with other scriptures. Don't forget, we are not promised tomorrow. God knew we would make mistakes and even have accidents. I look forward to doing a Bible study with anyone or group who disagrees with these last statements of mine.

Sincerely, and with love,

Tony Little

The smaller attacks began. An insurance company threatened me with a lawsuit for ruining a carpet. The ridiculous claim was untrue and frivolous. I prepared my court case, gathered evidence, showed it to my opponent and silenced them. I'm thankful for my friends who helped me with that dilemma.

Attacks continued for several months. One came from a preacher. I attended his church for a few months. Perhaps it was a rebuke, but it didn't resemble kindness. A couple in his church were having financial problems and were about to lose their home. I liked them and offered to help any way I could. I gave them some money and promised more if they would consider financial counseling. They didn't contact me about the counseling; I thought that was the end of it.

Their pastor requested a meeting. He was upset with me for wanting to counsel his members. I explained the couple didn't accept the offer, so no harm was done. I disagreed with him and replied, "If I become friends with your church members and want to give someone advice, that should be alright." He said, "No!" and I asked why. He stated he would be held accountable for his people and if anyone counseled them, it would be him. He was the preacher who said in a sermon, "You don't need counsel from anyone. The only one you need counsel from is Jesus Christ." We need counsel from others; it's in the Bible in many places.

I wondered why the preacher didn't like me. He glared and acted strange, as if he didn't trust me. Perhaps he remembered, I was writing this story and he felt intimidated. I didn't do anything to cause that. He made another accusation. Someone told him I made this remark; some of the Sunday School teachers in his church weren't qualified. He said that was strife. I said, "I don't recall making a statement like that. Perhaps someone misunderstood me."

We know when it's time to leave a church; that time had come. I told him, it wouldn't happen again. He didn't want me there; it was mutual. God sent me there for a reason; it was fulfilled. The last sermon I heard him preach stays in my mind. He said Christians should be peculiar and others should notice God in us. His sermons were powerful, but full of wrong traditions. He desires to raise the standard for himself and his congregation. God will provide advocates to help if he allows it. A masters degree can be problematic if obtained through the wrong traditions of men! It would be great if Bible college professors repented.

We struggle when doing our best. One reason we come to God as a child is, we desperately need his guidance. The main reason is Jesus declared, "Verily I say unto you, Whosoever shall not receive the kingdom of God as a little child, he shall not enter therein." (Mark 10:15) Despite your age, come to Him as a child; take His Word for it.

CHAPTER FOURTEEN

WHAT DID JESUS SAY ABOUT IT?

J esus declared, "He that speaketh of himself seeketh his own glory: but he that seeketh His glory that sent Him, the same is true, and no unrighteousness is in Him." (John 7:18) Only in Jesus Christ, can we find righteousness or be righteous. We should strive to be above reproach. This is perhaps the main qualification of a pastor or deacon.

(Mt. 10:26) "Fear them not therefore: for there is nothing covered, that shall not be revealed; and hid, that shall not be known." (Luke 8:17) "For nothing is secret, that shall not be made manifest; neither anything hid, that shall not be known and come abroad." In Luke 12:2–3 Jesus declared, "For there is nothing covered, that shall not be revealed; neither hid, that shall not be known. Therefore whatsoever ye have spoken in darkness shall be heard in the light; and that which ye have spoken in the ear in closets shall be proclaimed upon the housetops." Beware, God not only hears, but knows our thoughts.

Jesus does many signs and wonders. His wonders are in the sunrise, sunset, and in people who have His Spirit. What a sweet Spirit, and friend we have in Jesus! Our Creator is insulted when we seek signs and wonders. He doesn't have to prove anything, creation is proof enough. We must believe that He is, and that He rewards those who diligently seek Him. (Heb. 11:6 paraphrased)

Jesus said in Matthew 12:39, "...An evil and adulterous generation seeketh after a sign; and there shall no sign be given to it, but the sign of the prophet Jonah." (Luke 11:30) "...For as Jonah was a sign unto the Ninevites, so shall also the Son of Man be to this generation." Jesus refers to Himself as the Son of Man many times. He is the sign that through our faith, will show greater signs than any false prophet could. His signs are real. Seeking signs can lead us into deception!

In Mark 16:15–18, Jesus gave the command, "...Go ye into all the world, and preach the gospel to every creature. He that believeth and is baptized shall be saved; but he that believeth not shall be damned. And these signs shall follow them that believe; In My name shall they cast out devils; they shall speak with new tongues; They shall take up serpents; and if they drink any deadly thing, it shall not hurt them; they shall lay hands on the sick, and they shall recover." Jesus meant those who truly believe in Him would be protected. He didn't mean we should handle poisonous snakes and eat or drink something deadly. Jesus didn't contradict His Word. "Jesus said unto him, It is written again, Thou shalt not tempt the Lord thy God." (Mt. 4:7)

We shouldn't rejoice in the power we have over demons. (Luke 10:20) "...Notwithstanding in this rejoice not, that the spirits are subject unto you; but rather rejoice, because your names are written in heaven." His Word instructs; let each esteem others better than themselves. (paraphrasing Phil. 2:3) Look for the good in others. There is good and bad in everyone. What we look for, we will find.

Jesus said in Luke 14:11, "For whosoever exalteth himself shall be abased; and he that humbleth himself shall be exalted." Jesus knew, if we exalted ourselves, we would become prideful and create false doctrines. We shouldn't misuse the power given by the Holy Ghost.

Jesus declared in John 15:26, "...But when the Comforter is come, whom I will send unto you from the Father, even the Spirit of truth, which proceedeth from the Father He shall testify of me." The Holy Spirit is the Holy Ghost, Spirit of truth and the Comforter. He leads us to Jesus. He is more accessible than anyone and smarter.

In John 16:13–14 Jesus explains, "Howbeit when he, the Spirit of truth is come, he will guide you into all truth: for he shall not speak of himself; but whatsoever he shall hear, that shall he speak: and he will show you things to come. He shall glorify me: for He shall receive of mine, and shall show it unto you." God shows us the future sometimes.

The Holy Ghost is wonderful and much needed in our lives. The things He provides are awesome: power, comfort, signs, wonders and miracles. However, Jesus should be our main focus. Some follow the Holy Ghost, seeking signs and they adore false prophets. Others ignore religion because of all the nonsense and hypocrisy.

When God blesses us with plenty, it would be easy to love money and ignore God. Jesus declared in Mt. 6:24, "No man can serve two masters: for either he will hate the one and love the other; or else he will hold to the one, and despise the other. Ye cannot serve God and mammon." Mammon is money or wealth worshiped as a god. Worship God—not your things! Jesus made it plain, if we love our possessions, we hate God. How could we make it to heaven, worshiping false gods?

"Then said Jesus unto his disciples, If any man will come after me, let him deny himself, and take up his cross, and follow me. For whosoever shall save his life shall lose it: and whosoever will lose his life for my sake shall find it. For what is a man profited, if he shall gain the whole world, and lose his own soul? or what shall a man give in exchange for his soul? For the Son of man shall come in the glory of his Father with his angels; and then he shall reward every man according to his works." (Mt. 16: 24–27)

Jesus warned in Mt. 24:4, "Take heed that no man deceive you." In Mt. 24:11 Jesus declared, "And many false prophets shall rise, and shall deceive many." He also stated in Mt. 24:24, "...For there shall arise false Christs, and false prophets, and shall show great signs and wonders; insomuch that, if it were possible, they shall deceive the very elect." Notice Jesus did not say, except for the very elect.

(Mt. 7:21–23) "Not everyone that saith unto Me, Lord, Lord, shall enter into the kingdom of heaven; but he that doeth the will of My Father which is in heaven. Many will say to Me in that day, Lord, Lord, have we not prophesied in thy name? and in thy name have cast out devils? and in thy name done many wonderful works? And then will I profess unto them, I never knew you: depart from me, ye that work iniquity."

Jesus warned in Luke 6:26. "Woe unto you, when all men shall speak well of you! For so did their fathers to the false prophets." Why do you think people speak well of false prophets? It happens all the time. Some false teachers have a huge following and they're wealthy. There is a logical explanation why people like false prophets and speak well of them.

False prophets, no matter what style, put on a show. Most everyone enjoys entertainment. Some preachers tell others what they want to hear. Have you heard the expression, tickle their ears? Their doctrines make people feel good. If something sounds too good, it's probably false.

Preachers that teach the truth cause people to feel uncomfortable. God's Word brings conviction. The truth upsets people that don't want to repent of sin. The truth of His Bible goes against traditions of men. A lot of religious people would rather have feel good doctrines; therefore they speak well of the false prophets.

When we think about false prophets, we should not envision some strange or unusual looking person. Most false prophets look like one of us. A Sunday School teacher could be one, our pastor, our aunt or uncle who don't preach or teach. When we teach the Word of God wrong, it's the same as saying false things about God. I don't know how many false statements would cause someone to become a false prophet. It's dangerous to speak wrong about God or His Word, because Jesus is the Word. People speak well of false prophets because they don't realize what they are. However, this is beginning to change. Often, I meet Christians who read their Bible, and many are doctrinally sound.

Be careful who you listen to. Don't be in the category that Jesus mentioned, the blind leading the blind; both shall fall into a ditch. False prophets are blind to the truth. A follower or student is blind to the truth, if they are following false prophets.

In Luke 6:40 Jesus taught, "...but everyone that is perfect shall be as his master." A student is subject to his teacher and he follows him, but everyone needs to study for themselves. No one wants wrong teaching. In John 8:32, Jesus said this. "...And ye shall know the truth, and the truth shall make you free." Jesus taught His disciples in John 14:6, "...I am the way, the truth, and the life: no man cometh unto the Father, but by me." Hebrews 13:8 declares. "Jesus Christ the same yesterday, and today, and forever." Jesus doesn't change; the truth doesn't change.

The devil is a liar and deceiver. Look what Jesus told the Pharisees about the devil. "Ye are of your father the devil, and the lusts of your father ye will do. He was a murderer from the beginning, and abode not in the truth, because there is no truth in him. When he speaketh a lie, he speaketh of his own: for he is a liar and the father of it." (John 8:44) Demons follow the devil and tell lies. Guess what we do when we follow them? False teaching is lying. Liars don't go to heaven.

Wrong traditions of men are prevalent today, as they used to be; most people can't see it. They want to hear what sounds good! A Bible can be misused and make people believe things that are astounding. It's sad to see good people become religious and miss heaven.

Jesus declared in Matthew 15:3, "Why do ye also transgress the commandment of God by your tradition?" In Mark 7:13 Jesus said, "Making the Word of God of none effect through your tradition, which ye have delivered: and many such like things do ye." Man's wrong ideas about religious or spiritual things are traditions of men that negate the Word of God. They go against the Bible. Today, we have modern style Pharisees around us—in every religion.

I will paraphrase Jesus Christ in Mt. 15:6–9...You have made the commandments of God ineffective by your traditions. You hypocrites, Isaiah prophesied of you saying, These people draw near to me with their mouth, and they honor me with their talk; but their hearts are far away from Me. They worship me in vain, teaching for doctrines—the commandments of men. Jesus declared in Mt. 23:28 and in verse 33, (28) "Even so ye also outwardly appear righteous unto men, but within ye are full of hypocrisy and iniquity. (33) "Ye serpents, ye generation of vipers, how can ye escape the damnation of hell?"

The Pharisees and scribes were strict about their traditions of men. They added rules to God's laws—too difficult for them to keep. They wanted to appear Godly and holy. They honored themselves and their positions. The Pharisees were very religious; they remind me of our leaders in many churches today. The ones who follow them can become just as dogmatic.

We definitely have the modern day equivalent of the scribes and Pharisees. Did they add to, and take away from God's Word just like present-day religious people? They certainly did. Religious nonsense has been going on forever. If we add laws to God's laws, we're absurd.

Some don't love God and people. Loving God with all you have is the great commandment. The second commandment, love your neighbor as yourself, is similar to the first. All the law and prophets hang on these two. I am interpreting Mt. 22:37–40. Do these two and you'll do the rest.

Some preachers have two types of sermons: get saved and live righteous. That should be the main focus, but we need the whole story. When we're judged by God, we'll be ashamed if we haven't studied.

It astonishes me how much of the Bible is skipped or ignored. There is a tremendous amount of knowledge that would be helpful. Doesn't it make you wonder what the problem is? It's false prophets teaching what most people want, so they can be happy. Some are missing the truth.

Some preachers are mean; their sermons aren't delivered with love. A spirit of fear is driving people into condemnation. Romans 8:1 tells us this. "There is therefore now no condemnation to them which are in Christ Jesus, who walk not after the flesh, but after the Spirit." Preachers forget the goodness of God leads us to repentance.

Some people speak in tongues in churches without interpretation. The Bible conveys—we should not. I've heard others forbid people to speak or pray in an unknown tongue. The Bible says forbid them not to speak in tongues. Apostle Paul said he spoke in tongues more than all, and he wished everybody would. He taught against the misuse of tongues.

Paul said, "I would that ye all spake with tongues, but rather that ye prophesied: for greater is he that prophesieth than he that speaketh with tongues, except he interpret, that the church may receive edifying." (1 Cor. 14:5) Paul declares, "For if I pray in an unknown tongue, my spirit prayeth, but my understanding is unfruitful. What is it then? I will pray with the spirit, and I will pray with the understanding also: I will sing with the spirit, and I will sing with the understanding also." (1 Cor. 14:14–15) Paul explained praying in the Spirit well. "I thank my God, I speak with tongues more than ye all: Yet in the church, I had rather speak five words with my understanding, that by my voice I might teach others also, than ten thousand words in an unknown tongue." (1 Cor. 14:18–19)

Someday we won't need to pray in the Spirit; tongues will cease. When that which is perfect comes—Jesus, we will know as we are known and knowledge will vanish. When we see Him Face to face, we won't know in part but completely. We'll be mature and put away childish things. Study 1 Cor. 12–13–14. You'll know when tongues will cease and when knowledge vanishes. We'll see the results of faith in Jesus and experience the awesome day of redemption. *Father help us remain, continue and abide in your Son Jesus until that great day when He completes our salvation. I ask in the name of Jesus Christ.*

Some fall in the floor to receive from God, and they're instructed to do this. They don't realize—sometimes this is emotionalism. Other people believe, maybe it's written in the Bible that ushers should catch them. It isn't written in the King James Bible. I don't think we can locate this in any Bible, or none that are credible. However, they teach that our Heavenly Father makes people fall. We were taught how to fall; it came through mind control and witchcraft. When I fell, it was the power of suggestions and emotionalism; I didn't experience anything special. It's dangerous to mislead others and tell lies, especially about God and His precious—Holy Word.

Sometimes people are starving and refuse to kill an animal because they believe it's a god. They also believe it may be one of their ancestors reincarnated. Some people wonder which group of false prophets are worse. I don't see any difference. They won't make it to heaven if they don't repent. Hopefully, some will study and get the truth.

Every person's work will be revealed. The fire of God will test our works, good or bad. If our work remains, we'll be rewarded. If our work burns, we'll suffer loss, but be saved so as by fire. Please look at First

Corinthians chapter three. Nothing defiled will enter heaven. The fire of God will burn up our bad works. All who enter heaven will be saved in the end so as by fire. "For our God is a consuming fire." (Heb. 12:29) Remember fire purifies.

Some believe these scriptures mean it's impossible for a saved person to lose their salvation. It simply does not say that. If you get anything correct in the Bible, you should get salvation right. It saddens my heart how people misinterpret the Holy Bible. Please study to show yourselves approved to God. We should rightly divide the word of truth.

In 1 Cor. 5:5 we find this. "To deliver such a one unto Satan for the destruction of the flesh, that the spirit may be saved in the day of the Lord Jesus." Some believe this scripture means God will kill a Christian who backslides and take them to heaven. Many preachers teach this, but I don't think they would test the theory. Who would join their friends in horrible sins, hoping God would take them to heaven?

It amazes me how blatant are the misinterpretations of God's Word. God will approve of us if we study. What do you think will happen if we don't? Some are so certain of the eternal security doctrine, they believe this has to mean what they think it does. Some reside in the category called—unreachable. I pray that we're always teachable. "Wherefore let him that thinketh he standeth take heed lest he fall." (1 Cor. 10:12) Paul writes another caution in the same book, chapter nine verse twenty-seven. "But I keep under my body, and bring it into subjection: lest that by any means, when I have preached to others, I myself should be a castaway." The Bible isn't that hard to understand; a woman said once—just read it!

1 Cor. 5:5 isn't that difficult to interpret. Paul was writing to the Corinthians about a man committing fornication with his father's wife. He told those Christians, to remove this person from their assembly. He hoped that would stop any further corruption of the people. He hoped the man would repent and be saved.

That the spirit may be saved, means the possibility does exist. May means possibly or likely. It does not mean shall or will. If we used a dictionary when we study our Bible, many false teachings would disappear. Jesus explained how everyone must repent or perish.

(Luke 13:3) "I tell you, Nay: but, except ye repent, ye shall all likewise perish." The Bible makes it plain, fornicators don't go to heaven. Some teach that a truly saved, born-again person can backslide into sin, never repent, and make it to heaven. They say God kills and takes them to heaven. Horrible sinning in Christians isn't rewarded with an early departure to heaven. I wish someone would show me this in the Bible. Would anyone test the theory? I doubt it. Many teach things, they wouldn't try, like having eternal life through murder and suicide.

There is no end to false teachings about the most important doctrine of all. The teaching on God's free gift, salvation—is the most important doctrine. This teaching is under more attack than any doctrine. Why do you think this is? Could it be Satan wants people to get it wrong so they will spend eternity with him? I think so. The Bible warns about people falling away, and it's happening. Intelligent, highly trained educated people lean to their own understanding. They are like the unlearned, and will not acknowledge God or His Holy Word!

Please study salvation with me. Do we really want to know the truth? Help me if I'm wrong on any subject. This old teacher doesn't esteem himself better than anyone else. I consider others better, greater and smarter than me. I'm teachable and love being taught. Fellowship with Christians is helpful. Good friends will be there for us if we need help; we can be there for them. There is strength in numbers and safety in a multitude of counsel.

If you're looking for a church, I know one that understands love. They teach faith and works doctrines correctly. This enables them to teach the truth about salvation. The name is Providence Church of the Living God. The church is located two miles west of the Old Mountain Road on highway 70 in Iredell County near Statesville N.C. It's an excellent little church; please visit!

God doesn't care what our religion is; He cares about us and what is in our hearts. God wants us to tell people about His Son Jesus and see Him Face to face in heaven. We should make sure we have salvation. Don't have a false sense of security. Bogus assurance is not going to give us peace. Only the truth does that. Be free from untruths and false teachings common in religions. None of us are as smart as all of us combined. We could study together and be benefited.

We'll have a genuine assurance of salvation while following Jesus Christ. We will love, fear Him and at the same time, be anxious for nothing. Someone said; we are saved by faith alone. I say; see if this lines up with God's Word. Don't put your trust in me or anyone else; trust God. *Father, please show me where I might be wrong, in Jesus name.*

CHAPTER FIFTEEN

ASSURANCE OF YOUR SALVATION

S alvation is the most important doctrine in the Bible. It is the gift of
God. It's referred to more than once as a free gift. No one is good
enough to earn this gift. Once we receive it, there are some things we
must do.

Salvation should be thoroughly understood; however, it's probably the
least understood doctrine. False teachings are the reason. They deceive
many who need to know the truth—not a half truth. Why are there so
many different ideas about salvation? I'm sure there is only one way that
works, Jesus Christ. People look for an easier way, one that eliminates any
work. No one can change God's plan of salvation. Many have tried—none
were successful!

(Proverbs 14:12) "There is a way which seemeth right unto a man; but
the end thereof are the ways of death." Jesus gives rest and peace. (Mt.
11:30) "For my yoke is easy, and my burden is light." It's possible most
believe it's difficult to have it easy following Christ. All Christians suffer
persecution at times, but suffer more if they don't follow Him. We have
many rewards in this life and heaven—if we follow Jesus.

When people don't surrender to Christ, they make the way difficult—
they make it impossible. If we are doing the best we can to obey and follow
Him, we have surrendered. A common theme in false teachings is this:
they sound good or easy. We must make sure teachings line up with His

Word. Surrender doesn't mean we are perfect. If we had to live in sinless perfection to arrive in heaven, no one would.

(1 John 1:9) "...If we confess our sins, He is faithful and just to forgive us our sins, and to cleanse us from all unrighteousness." That is true, but we don't have a license to sin. Surrendering, is allowing Jesus to reign or rule us as Lord and King. That means we sincerely—follow and obey Him. If we believe in Jesus, we'll do what He tells us. If we don't obey Jesus, we don't really believe in Him. Some teach that we don't have to do anything but believe in Him. They say things like: You are trying to add to His grace. You are saying that grace is not enough, or is not sufficient. You are saying we have to earn our way to heaven by works. Look closely at my writings; I do not say any such thing. I am teaching what God's Word declares about His salvation. People are notorious at misunderstanding others.

Demons use people to tell lies about God's free gift of salvation. I believe they use religious people more than others. It's rare that unsaved people discuss these things. It's the religious crowd that demons use to seduce others into the—too good to be true beliefs. What we need is old fashioned Bible study. I couldn't write this without extensive Bible study, prayer and meditating on His Word.

The devil and his demons cause much confusion, doubt, fear, and false teachings. God's salvation (the most important doctrine) has been distorted by demons. When thoughts don't line up with the Bible, don't listen to them. Even though the pleasant stories were handed down from one generation to the next, don't listen. Some teachings sound too good to be true—because they are false. If they don't line up with God's Word, avoid them.

Jesus Christ stated this in Mt. 5:20. "For I say unto you, That except your righteousness shall exceed the righteousness of the scribes and Pharisees, ye shall in no case enter into the kingdom of heaven." Yes, we must be righteous! Some teach the opposite.

Jesus allows some to teach a little false doctrine and make it to heaven. (Matthew 5:19) "Whosoever therefore shall break one of these least commandments, and shall teach men so, he shall be called the least in the kingdom of heaven: but whosoever shall do and teach them, the same shall be called great in the kingdom of heaven." Don't barely get by and be called "the least." You may not make it.

What would happen if we broke some of the main commandments, or even one? We don't know when we would cross the line, becoming a false prophet. We're not perfect, but we shouldn't attempt to justify our sins. Get everything as correct as you possibly can. People should understand salvation. There are many fairy tales about that subject.

This chapter will cause conviction. Conviction is a good thing if we repent. Working on this project helped me repent of many things. Please don't let conviction turn into denial, hate, or condemnation. It can happen.

(Romans 8:1) "There is therefore now no condemnation to them which are in Christ Jesus, who walk not after the flesh, but after the Spirit." (Romans 8:6) "...For to be carnally minded is death; but to be spiritually minded is life and peace." I beg you to choose life. If we walk in the flesh, we are carnal and it can kill.

I heard an interesting sermon. The preacher was old and struggled with the delivery of his message. Soon after he began speaking, a most unusual teaching proceeded from him. He said, "Some people believe that people will spend eternity in a place called hell. Can someone please show me where that is located in the Bible? The Bible does mention a place called the lake of fire. It was created for the devil and his crowd. Death and hell were cast into the lake of fire." At times in the Bible, hell means the grave.

I believe the man was implying death and hell would be destroyed. Death and the grave will be destroyed. The lake of fire is everlasting. He didn't elaborate, but went on to another subject. I'll show where this is located in the Bible.

Jesus declared this in Mt. 5:22 in the last part of the verse. "...but whosoever shall say, Thou fool, shall be in danger of hell fire." He also said in Mt. 5:30, in the last part, "...for it is profitable for thee that one of thy members should perish, and not that thy whole body should be cast into hell."

155

Jesus declared in Mt. 10:28, "...but rather fear Him which is able to destroy both soul and body in hell." He stated in Mt. 11:23, "And thou, Capernaum, which art exalted unto heaven, shall be brought down to hell." In Luke 12:5 He said, "...But I will forewarn you whom ye shall fear: Fear him, which after he hath killed hath power to cast into hell; yea, I say unto you, Fear him." I hope the preacher realizes, people will spend eternity in a literal place called hell. (the lake of fire)

Jesus stated in Luke 16:23, "And in hell he lift up his eyes, being in torments, and seeth Abraham afar off, and Lazarus in his bosom." Jesus explained in Mt. 25:41–46. (41) "...Depart from me, ye cursed, into everlasting fire, prepared for the devil and his angels:" Look closely at (46). "And these shall go away into everlasting punishment but the righteous into life eternal." Look in Rev. 20:14–15; we find this. "...And death and hell were cast into the lake of fire. This is the second death. And whosoever was not found written in the book of life was cast into the lake of fire."

The second death is a spiritual death and not physical. In hell, people never expire. They suffer for eternity. It's not God's desire that anyone goes there. He allows our free will to decide where we spend eternity.

Look at John 3:16. "...For God so loved the world, that He gave His only begotten Son, that whosoever believeth in Him should not perish, but have everlasting life." He said in Mt. 5:3, "Blessed are the poor in spirit: for theirs is the kingdom of heaven." (Mt. 5:10–12) "Blessed are they which are persecuted for righteousness sake: for theirs is the kingdom of heaven. Blessed are ye, when men shall revile you, and persecute you, and shall say all manner of evil against you falsely, for My sake. Rejoice, and be exceeding glad: for great is your reward in heaven: for so persecuted they the prophets which were before you." Jesus said in Mt. 10:22 in the last part, "but he that endureth to the end shall be saved." In Mt. 24:13 He said, "But he that shall endure unto the end, the same shall be saved."

(Eph. 2:8–9) "For by grace are ye saved through faith; and that not of yourselves: It is the gift of God: Not of works, lest any man should boast." Not of works means, not derived from works. Eph. 2:9 is where well meaning, good people miss it. The verses before and after are proof that works of faith in Jesus—is a part of salvation.

True faith contains works. (James 2:17–18) "Even so faith, if it hath not works, is dead, being alone." (James 2:18) "Yea, a man may say, Thou hast faith, and I have works: show me thy faith without thy works, and I will show thee my faith by my works."

(James 2:22) "Seest thou how faith wrought with his works, and by works was faith made perfect?" (24) "Ye see then how that by works a man is justified, and not by faith only." (26) "For as the body without the spirit is dead, so faith without works is dead also." Faith without works doesn't exist! The Bible teaches; we are justified by the blood of Christ, His grace, our works, words and by our faith! Faith has substance and evidence. (paraphrasing Heb. 11:1) We can't have enough works to earn salvation; however, after we receive this free gift from God, we change. If there is no evidence of something, it doesn't exist. Works are the evidence of salvation, not the cause of. If you are confused on the works doctrine, don't feel bad; most of us have been this way—even teachers and preachers.

I have a friend who believes works has nothing to do with salvation. That teaching is a false philosophy. Jesus said in John 10:27, My sheep follow Me. If we follow Him, we won't perish or lose salvation. We must meet the requirements of conditional promises God has in His Word. Jesus Christ told us to: receive the kingdom of heaven as a little child; do the will of our Heavenly Father; become a new creature, let old things pass away and all things become new; love the brethren; love our enemies; love God and obey His commandments; endure chastening and endure to the end. How can people disagree with that? These things are written in the Bible.

Some say if we stop following Jesus Christ, we were never saved. We have seen and heard of people who follow Jesus for years, and give up. Salvation can only be judged by God. It's my conviction, that some fall away and stay that way. They had salvation, but chose to give it up.

A preacher said, "You can't lose your salvation no matter how hard you try." Who would try? What happens to saved people who commit the unpardonable sin? In the flesh it's impossible to do right. The only way to accomplish this is our faith in Jesus. He taught in John 3:3. "...Verily, verily, I say unto thee, Except a man be born again, he cannot see the kingdom of God." In 1 John 3:9 we find this. "Whosoever is born of God doth not commit sin; for His seed remaineth in him: and he cannot sin, because he is born of God." Look closely at this.

People say, our spirit goes to heaven, not our sinful flesh. They say we'll get a glorified body. They're correct. They are incorrect in using this to declare, works of the flesh can't send people to hell. This is contrary to Bible teaching. A born-again spirit can't sin; the flesh sure can. Look in Galatians, chapters five and six, and in 1 Cor. 6:9–10 to dismiss this false teaching. Paul teaches, those who do the works of the flesh, shall never inherit the kingdom of God. We struggle after we're saved. If we confess our sins, He will definitely forgive us.

Gal. 2:20 says, "I am crucified with Christ: nevertheless I live; yet not I, but Christ liveth in me: and the life which I now live in the flesh I live by the faith of the Son of God who loved me, and gave Himself for me." It would be difficult without His indwelling Spirit—His Presence.

Jesus declared in Luke 7:50, "...Thy faith hath saved thee; go in peace." (Luke 18:42) "And Jesus said unto him, Receive thy sight: thy faith hath saved thee." Our faith is counted for righteousness. "For what saith the scripture? Abraham believed God, and it was counted unto him for righteousness. Now to him that worketh is the reward not reckoned of grace, but of debt. But to him that worketh not, but believeth on him that justifieth the ungodly, his faith is counted for righteousness." (Rom. 4:3–5) Paul made it plain; we can't earn salvation by works of the law. This fact doesn't contradict that our works of faith in Jesus Christ are necessary. Titus 1:16 declares, "...They profess that they know God; but in works they deny Him, being abominable, and disobedient, and unto every good work reprobate." Paul's letter said to Titus—maintain good works.

(Rev. 3:5) "He that overcometh, the same shall be clothed in white raiment; and I will not blot out his name out of the book of life, but I will confess his name before My Father, and before His angels." When we overcome things, it takes action, the works of faith; it's bearing fruit.

(Mt. 10:22) "And ye shall be hated of all men for My name's sake: but he that endureth to the end shall be saved." We are saved by the grace of God through faith. Salvation is a two part, lifetime process. God does His part. We should do ours. Please overcome and endure so Jesus will not blot your name out of the book of life.

Please don't misinterpret scriptures. If we do, we take away from the words of the Bible. We all make mistakes. If we misinterpret a lot of scriptures, we'll be in extreme danger. Inferior translations have taken words out of their Bibles. The problem is—when they take away from the words by changing the meaning of the original translation. Many people take away from the words by misinterpreting the King James Version. This is extremely dangerous.

Look closely at Rev. 22:19. "And if any man shall take away from the words of the book of this prophecy, God shall take away his part out of the book of life, and out of the holy city, and from the things which are written in this book." Someone told me this, "You can't lose your salvation; God will just take your part out of the book of life." How could God take away our part without taking away our name? Most everyone agrees the names written in the book of life are the names of saved people. (Rev. 20:15) "...And whosoever was not found written in the book of life was cast into the lake of fire."

I've heard people say; you can't lose your salvation, because the devil can't cross over the blood line in the hand of Jesus to get you, or he would have to get saved. I could say; you can't lose your salvation because a goat can't jump over a ten foot fence. My bad analogy would make about as much sense as that one.

Someone said; you can't lose your salvation, because blood makes a permanent stain. The fact is, it doesn't always stain. Even if blood left a permanent stain, what does that have to do with whether we can lose our salvation or not? Can anyone say—bad analogy?

People declare, once we're born with the natural birth, we can't become unborn; and once we're born-again (saved),we can't become unborn. It sounds like an (apples and oranges) wrong comparison. The supernatural birth is completely different than the natural. Why do people use bad analogies to explain the most important doctrine of all? They use scriptures to support once saved always saved that aren't on the same subject. Someone showed me in Rom. 8:37–39 that proved nothing is able to separate anyone from God's love.

God won't stop loving us; He is love. After God pours out His wrath on people, He'll still love them. It's in the Bible; be angry and sin not. God can be angry but doesn't sin. Without punishment, who would do right? If you study Romans chapter eight, you'll see, God will always love us. It doesn't imply we can't give up salvation.

This is the last part of Heb. 13:5. "...I will never leave thee nor forsake thee." God is omnipresent. This means He is everywhere, at the same time. (Psalm 139:7–10) "Whither shall I go from thy Spirit? Or whither shall I flee from thy presence? If I ascend up into heaven, thou art there: if I make my bed in hell, behold, thou art there. If I take the wings of the morning, and dwell in the uttermost parts of the sea; even there shall thy hand lead me, and thy right hand shall hold me." God is everywhere, it's impossible for Him to leave or forsake us. People misinterpret this to mean once saved, always saved! God isn't in unsaved people, but He is with them. "Behold, I stand at the door and knock..." (Rev. 3:20)

Jesus declared in John 10:27–29, "My sheep hear My voice, and I know them, and they follow Me: And I give unto them eternal life; and they shall never perish, neither shall any man pluck them out of My hand. My Father, which gave them me, is greater than all; and no man is able to pluck them out of My Father's hand." They follow me, makes the promise conditional. Some say, we don't have to do anything; salvation is not of works. It is through works. We must follow Jesus Christ!

Words have different meanings. Some have a few short definitions that mean basically the same thing. Some think whereby means because. (Eph. 4:30) "And grieve not the Holy Spirit of God, whereby ye are sealed unto the day of redemption." If whereby meant because, this scripture would support the doctrine, once you're saved, you are always saved. The true meaning of Eph. 4:30 helps us understand how we've been wrong about other scriptures. Knowing God's Word gives assurance of salvation... "The fear of the Lord is the beginning of knowledge: but fools despise wisdom and instruction." (Prov. 1:7)

Whereby means by what, how, by which and by means of which. It means the way or how we're sealed. Not grieving the Holy Spirit of God is how we're sealed and won't give up salvation. I've studied all the sealed verses. None support once saved, always saved. If we grieve the Holy Spirit by willful sinning, we must repent. Grieve means intense sorrow! Don't grieve Him!

(Jer. 3:14–15) "...Turn, O backsliding children, saith the Lord; for I am married unto you: and I will take you one of a city, and two of a family, and I will bring you to Zion. And I will give you pastors according to mine heart, which shall feed you with knowledge and understanding." We need preachers who teach sound doctrine. Look in Hosea 4:6, in the first part. "My people are destroyed for lack of knowledge..." Find a pastor who fears God and teaches properly.

I don't believe salvation is easily lost. God strives as long as it takes, if we will accept Him someday. He knows the future. If a person doesn't accept Jesus, at some point, God turns them over to a reprobate mind, to allow whatever they want. Don't harden your heart.

Look at 1 Cor. 2:14. "But the natural man receiveth not the things of the Spirit of God for they are foolishness unto him: neither can he know them, because they are spiritually discerned." Unsaved people don't have God's Spirit in them.

(1 John 4:4–16) "Ye are of God, little children, and have overcome them: because greater is He that is in you, than he that is in the world. They are of the world: therefore speak they of the world, and the world heareth them. We are of God: He that knoweth God heareth us; he that is not of God heareth not us. Hereby know we the spirit of truth, and the spirit of error. Beloved, let us love one another: for love is of God; and everyone that loveth is born of God, and knoweth God. He that loveth not knoweth not God: for God is love. In this was manifested the love of God toward us, because that God sent His only begotten Son into the world, that we might live through Him.

Herein is love, not that we loved God, but that He loved us, and sent his Son to be the propitiation for our sins. Beloved, if God so loved us, we ought also to love one another. No man hath seen God at any time. If we love one another, God dwelleth in us, and His love is perfected in us. Hereby know we that we dwell in Him, and He in us, because He hath given us of His Spirit. And we have seen and do testify that the Father sent the Son to be the Savior of the world. Whosoever shall confess that Jesus is the Son of God, God dwelleth in him, and he in God. And we have known and believed the love that God hath to us. God is love; and he that dwelleth in love dwelleth in God, and God in him." *Thank you Father for your salvation and your indwelling Spirit, in Jesus name.*

In John 14:16–17 we find this. "...And I will pray the Father, and He shall give you another Comforter, that He may abide with you forever; Even the Spirit of truth; whom the world cannot receive, because it seeth Him not, neither knoweth Him: but ye know Him; for He dwelleth with you, and shall be in you." Anyone who accepts Jesus knows the Spirit of God lives in them. (John 14:20) "At that day ye shall know that I am in My Father, and ye in Me, and I in you."

(Rom. 8:16) "The Spirit itself beareth witness with our spirit, that we are the children of God." The Spirit Himself, Jesus said this in John 15:1–10. "I am the true vine, and My Father is the husbandman. Every branch in Me that beareth not fruit He taketh away: and every branch that beareth fruit, He purgeth it, that it may bring forth more fruit. Now ye are clean through the word which I have spoken unto you. Abide in Me, and I in you. As the branch cannot bear fruit of itself, except it abide in the vine; no more can ye, except ye abide in Me. I am the vine, ye are the branches: He that abideth in Me, and I in him, the same bringeth forth much fruit: for without Me ye can do nothing. If a man abide not in Me, he is cast forth as a branch, and is withered; and men gather them, and cast them into the fire, and they are burned. If ye abide in Me, and My words abide in you, ye shall ask what ye will and it shall be done unto you. Herein is my Father glorified, that ye bear much fruit; so shall ye be My disciples. As the Father hath loved Me, so have I loved you: continue ye in my love. If ye keep my commandments, ye shall abide in my love; even as I have kept my Father's commandments, and abide in his love." We have to obey Jesus to abide in Him. Abide means to remain, and reside.

Jesus said in Rev. 3:15–17, "...I know thy works, that thou art neither cold nor hot: I would thou wert cold or hot. So then because thou art lukewarm, and neither cold nor hot, I will spew thee out of my mouth. Because thou sayest, I am rich, and increased with goods, and have need of nothing; and knowest not that thou art wretched, and miserable, and poor, and blind, and naked:" Jesus was rebuking the Laodiceans. He said nothing good about them. He explained, they were lost and needed to accept Him. They thought they had salvation and needed nothing. They attempted to enter Him the wrong way; He spewed them out. There is no such thing as a lukewarm Christian; they're lost and need salvation.

Some think they can't do any wrong. Others believe after they accept salvation, it doesn't matter what they do. Others say, I believe in Jesus and that is all I have to do. Take heed lest you fall. Jesus made it clear; people in Him can fall away. Jesus declared, every branch in Me that doesn't bear fruit—He shall take away. A preacher that believed in once saved always saved had another view of John chapter fifteen. He said, we can't put too much significance in a parable. Everything Jesus Christ said was significant! God teaches with perfection.

Some say, it's not our salvation to lose; it's God's. The Bible says, work out your own salvation with fear and trembling. When a gift is given, the recipient has ownership. Some say, you can't give the gift back. We can throw away a gift or destroy it and I believe we can do the same with our salvation. Rather than use analogies to prove this point, let's use scriptures. Please study what I teach; it comes from a reliable source. (the Bible) I'm trying my best to properly interpret His Word.

Jesus told His disciples in John 15:3, "...Now ye are clean through the word which I have spoken unto you." He meant they were saved. He wanted them to remain in Him, because He knew they could give up or lose their salvation.

163

Jesus declared this in Rev. 22:12–13. "And behold I come quickly; and my reward is with Me, to give every man according as his work shall be. I am Alpha and Omega, the beginning and the end, the first and the last." John said this in the next verse. "Blessed are they that do His commandments, that they may have right to the tree of life, and may enter in through the gates into the city." (conditional promise)

Apostle Peter wrote two letters to saved people. (1 Peter 1:5) "Who are kept by the power of God through faith unto salvation ready to be revealed in the last time." Who are kept means, who are sealed by not grieving the Holy Spirit. By the power of God means His love and mercy. (grace) Don't worry about God doing His part. Faith is our part. If it was impossible to lose our salvation, we wouldn't be concerned with being kept, or abiding. To be revealed in the last time is the judgment. (1 Peter 1:9) "...Receiving the end of your faith, even the salvation of your souls." This verse means our salvation is completed when we keep our faith to the end. There is an expression, "keep the faith." It is biblical.

(Eph. 4:30) "And grieve not the Holy Spirit of God, whereby ye are sealed unto the day of redemption." If we grieve the Holy Spirit by willful sinning, we can unseal, or lose our salvation. Heb. 10:26 makes it clear. "For if we sin willfully after that we have received the knowledge of the truth, there remaineth no more sacrifice for sins." Willful sinning is dangerous; there is a solution, stop. Ask God to forgive; hopefully, He will. (The key is stop.) *Thanks Lord for helping us overcome sin.*

We tend to backslide. God forgives us, if we ask and repent, because His mercy endures forever. If we knew how much sin we could get away with, we might try. God won't reveal where that line is; He didn't intend for us to live like that. When we sin, let's make sure it's not intentional.

In Peter's second letter he warned people to add to their faith. He stated, if they didn't have virtue, knowledge, self-control, perseverance, godliness, kindness and love—they would be in profound trouble. He explained if they didn't do these things, they might lose their salvation. 2 Peter 1:1–11 explains this. 2 Peter 2:20–22 is another proof—we can lose salvation. We find proof in 1 Cor. 15:1–2, John 15:1–2, Rom. 11:19–22, and

2 John 1:8–9. There are other references in the Bible. We should look at 1 John 3:15. "Whosoever hateth his brother is a murderer: and ye know that no murderer hath eternal life abiding in him." If we hate someone, salvation is not remaining in us. We need to rededicate our lives to Christ and repent quickly. Sometimes we have to restore our salvation. Remember, the Bible says, work out your own salvation.

Paul explains in Romans, we are justified by faith and not by deeds of the law. He was writing about the works of the law and not the works of faith. (Rom. 3:27–28) "Where is boasting then? It is excluded. By what law? Of works? Nay: but by the law of faith. Therefore we conclude that a man is justified by faith without the deeds of the law." Deeds of the law and works of the law are the same. "for by the works of the law shall no flesh be justified." This is the last part of Gal. 2:16. Look at James 2:24. "Ye see then how that by works a man is justified, and not by faith only." James wrote about the works of faith, and not about the deeds, or works, of the law. There is a big difference in the two types of works.

There is no contradiction in Paul's or James' writings. The Bible tells of good works, bad works, works of the flesh, dead works, works or deeds of the law, and the works of faith. We must do the works of faith in Jesus Christ. It's made clear in His Word, if we try to earn salvation with good works, we're using works of the law, dead works. God knew this was impossible for us. That is why He died for us. He knew if He would suffer and die a horrible death, maybe, just maybe, we would suffer a little and live for Him.

If we live only for ourselves, we most likely have made ourselves into false gods. This can happen to anyone, and we know better. God put His Word in our hearts and minds. He taught, by their fruits we would know them. Jesus meant, by their actions. He was talking about false prophets and Christians. Overcome false teachings or you could miss heaven. I've heard it said; religion sends people to hell. It's the most powerful tool Satan has to destroy us. Religion can brainwash anyone.

Most believe Paul wrote Hebrews, and so do I. Look at Hebrews 5:9. "...And being made perfect, He became the author of eternal salvation—unto all them that obey Him:" Do you believe this scripture is a conditional promise? All Bible verses about salvation are conditional. We must stop following traditions of men that teach against the Word of God. Are you beginning to see how we've been taught wrong?

Modern day scribes and Pharisees are false prophets. Please study the book of Hebrews in chapters five and six, the last part of five and the first part of six. Paul was teaching Christians about Jesus being the high priest. He said he had much to say, but it was difficult to explain. He said people had become dull of hearing. After they got saved, the devil came to steal the word sown in their hearts. We must keep up the study, or the evil ones steal His Word from us. The devil wants us confused; he hopes to drag us into hell. Do not allow this. Greater is He that is in you, than he that is in the world—if you're saved.

Confusion blinds some and they can't see the truth. They're dogmatic about their false doctrines. Dogmatic means strongly opinionated in an arrogant manner without proof. I've been like that most of my life. We need strong opinions with humility and proof. (God's Holy Word)

Paul said, by this time, you should be teachers but instead you have need of being taught. Paul knew they needed the milk of God's Word. (basic or elementary teachings) He knew they would struggle with the meat or deep things of God. He decided to take them deeper. He said we will do this if God permits. Paul described them as enlightened. He said they had tasted the heavenly gift. (salvation) He said they were made partakers of the Holy Ghost—tasted the good Word of God, and the powers of the world to come. An unsaved person isn't a partaker of the Holy Spirit. He won't enter a lost person.

Paul was writing to Christians. Study scriptures that contain partake or partakers. They refer to the first definition of partake. Paul declared in Hebrews, chapter six; it's impossible for saved people to be renewed again to repentance, if they fall away. He said they—crucify to themselves, the Son of God afresh and put Him to an open shame. The Bible said—crucify to themselves; no one can crucify Christ again!

This type of fall away is when a person gives up salvation and commits the—only sin that God will not forgive. Blaspheming the Holy Ghost is the unpardonable sin: not divorce, murder, adultery, etc. Jesus said in Mark 3:28–29, "...Verily I say unto you, All sins shall be forgiven unto the sons of men, and blasphemies wherewith soever they shall blaspheme: But he that shall blaspheme against the Holy Ghost hath never forgiveness, but is in danger of eternal damnation:" First John 5:16 says, "There is a sin unto death:" We fall away sometimes. The deadly type of falling away is when we never repent. If we continue in the sins of the flesh, called the works of the flesh, we could be heading toward the unpardonable sin, blasphemy. Some sins are unto death. The unpardonable sin leads to the worst one, the second death.

If we don't work out our own salvation with fear and trembling, we are headed in the wrong direction. We shouldn't believe we have gone too far or too long in sin. When sin abounds, God's grace more abounds. God's mercy endures forever. I wouldn't advise anyone to willfully sin and procrastinate. Stop and repent; sincerely ask and He will forgive!

Rest assured, we shouldn't think it's too late. We can't judge this. (1 John 1:9) "If we confess our sins, He is faithful and just to forgive us our sins, and to cleanse us from all unrighteousness." Look at First John 1:8. "If we say that we have no sin, we deceive ourselves, and the truth is not in us." God's grace is so awesome; we don't have to live in sinless perfection. We should strive to do our best. His Spirit helps us in this journey called life, if we listen and obey.

Jesus declared in Mt. 5:19, "Whosoever therefore shall break one of these least commandments, and shall teach men so, he shall be called the least in the kingdom of heaven: but whosoever shall do and teach them the same shall be called great in the kingdom of heaven." We should always strive to follow Jesus Christ and not live in condemnation. The previous verse helps me understand His grace.

We can have assurance of salvation. The only way is to follow Jesus and obey Him the best we can. Jesus said, "I am the way." It's dangerous to have assurance through a false teaching. Commandments that surround His salvation, are the greatest. Please teach them correctly.

James 3:1 says, "My brethren, be not many masters, knowing that we shall receive the greater condemnation." Teachers and preachers should be careful when teaching about God or His Word! We will be held to a higher standard. We must seek His will, and get things right! If people see clearly how—once saved, always saved is false, they might see other false teachings. Some say it's impossible for saved people to backslide and remain that way. They say if someone does, they weren't truly saved. Only God can judge a person's salvation; we can't.

Jesus implied we can be deceived and many will. He said if possible, the very elect. He didn't say except for the very elect. I'm paraphrasing Mt.24:24. This is important. "Wherefore let him that thinketh he standeth take heed lest he fall." (1 Cor. 10:12) If we think we've arrived, we're committing the sin of pride. I've humbled myself with pride. It can embarrass and humiliate. If someone doesn't ask God for forgiveness and stop pride, it could put them at the great white throne of judgment. Pride, selfishness, indifference, unforgiveness, or hate could place us in hell forever!

Some say it's possible for a saved person to backslide horribly, never repent, and still make it to heaven. They say God kills those people and takes them to heaven. Jesus declared in Luke 13:5, "...I tell you, Nay: but, except ye repent, ye shall all likewise perish." The baptism of repentance should be an everyday experience.

Some state, you couldn't lose salvation no matter how hard you tried. Who would try? It amazes me how other false teachings follow the salvation doctrine. We won't lose our salvation if we follow Jesus to the end of our life. Why can't some make this elaboration? Who would believe we could sin horribly and get to heaven quicker? Christians have more sense, even those who teach it. It's time to leave deception.

A person having assurance of their salvation is important. If we don't fully understand it, we may not have it. Demons put thoughts in our minds and lie about salvation. People teach others about these lies. These false teachings, or doctrines can lead others into a false sense of security. It really doesn't matter who or how many teach salvation wrong; it is dangerous. Make sure teachings line up with God's Word!

I've heard of a teaching called eternal security. People state, it is impossible for a person to lose their salvation. They misinterpret a lot of scriptures in the Bible. I have made the same mistakes all my life, because I didn't study.

Thank God, I found the truth at age fifty-four. We can't make the way easier than it is! Everyone has troubles. Christians have it easier—than lost people. "Why do the heathen rage and the people imagine a vain thing?" (Psalm 2:1) Christians have peace no matter what troubles they encounter. The Bible describes it as having the peace that surpasses all understanding; it only comes from God.

We must hunger and thirst after righteousness to obtain it. This came to me during Bible study and prayer. (Mt. 22:37–40) "Thou shalt love the Lord thy God with all thy heart, and with all thy soul, and with all thy mind. This is the first and great commandment. And the second is like the first, thou shalt love thy neighbor as thyself. On these two commandments hang all the law and the prophets." Jesus knows if we focus on the two main commandments, we'll do the others as well.

The stronger a person's faith is, the closer they are to Christ. The closer we are, the more assurance we have. When evil thoughts come we have to change the subject in our minds and think on good things. It's necessary, because our adversary the devil is like a roaring lion; he seeks anyone he may devour. If you are saved, greater is He that is in you than he that is in the world.

If we would elaborate, we wouldn't be guilty of half truths. The whole truth is—once we're saved, we won't lose salvation, if we follow Jesus and obey Him the best we can, to the end. God knows our heart. He knows if we're sincere. When we say a person can't lose their salvation, we tell a half truth. Often a half truth is deception; it is a lie!

The truth is incredibly important in a court of law. We are asked to place our hand on a Bible and swear to tell the truth, the whole truth and nothing but the truth. The great truth about God's salvation is the most important truth of all.

CONCLUSION

W hen I said Karen died four days after the last false prophet left town, I meant a certain group left. If there are more, hopefully they will change. False prophets are in every religion and people speak well of them. They like feel good doctrines, even ones that sound too good to be true. Obviously, their followers agree with them.

Karen left churches because she didn't want to be taught how to take away from words in the Bible. She didn't want her part taken out of the book of life, the holy city or from the things written in God's Word.

Karen thought full gospel churches interpreted the Bible accurately. However, she was unaware they added things and brought plagues on themselves. I'm paraphrasing Rev. 22:18.

We can focus too much on religion, while slowly losing love for people. Family, friends and work can be neglected. Why do some love church more than anything? God should be first. Maybe this is why. (Heb. 10:25) "Not forsaking the assembling of ourselves together, as the manner of some is..." Please read this chapter. The implication is, if we don't assemble in church we might lose our salvation—perhaps not. The Bible didn't say church; some assemble in their homes to study and it works. Many are home bound because of health problems. Salvation is not based on church attendance. Religion can be a pathway that leads to Jesus; but Jesus is the only way that leads to eternal life. If we can't find a good church, we should assemble somewhere and study.

The last part of Hebrews chapter ten says, "Cast not away therefore your confidence, which hath great recompense of reward. For ye have need of patience, that, after ye have done the will of God, ye might receive the promise. For yet a little while, and he that shall come will come, and will not tarry. Now the just shall live by faith: but if any man draw back, my soul shall have no pleasure in him. But we are not of them who draw back unto perdition; but of them that believe unto the saving of the soul." (Heb. 10:35–39)

Without church attendance or some type of assembly, there is a danger of backsliding to eternity in the wrong place. That is why some love their church more than a spouse, or anyone. We should love people and our church, without putting church first. That is the proper balance.

Many churches lead to the way, Jesus. Some believe their religion is the only way that leads to heaven. This is wrong. Many pathways lead to Jesus Christ. Different religions acknowledge the cleansing power of the blood of Jesus. God wants a changed heart and attitude toward Him. (born-again) Our Father in heaven doesn't have a religion. When we criticize religions; remember, we have problems in our own.

Please your spouse by choosing a church of their preference. We could show them, where some teachings are incorrect. If a church is teaching mostly good, we could overlook mistakes and keep our marriage together. If your marriage is strong, you could attend different churches. Some do this and it works for them.

Some churches have too much false teaching and should be avoided. Love your spouse more than a religion. They are like your own flesh. Remember, "they shall be one flesh." (Gen. 2:24) If we hurt them, we hurt ourselves. Don't let religion cause your divorce.

If we aren't loving people as we should, then we don't love God properly. The Bible makes it plain; we must love everyone. Study the book of John, also First, Second and Third John. They explain how we should love.

Religious people love their self-imposed righteousness. They adore the building where they worship. The worship of wood or stone is idolatry. Anything can become an idol, even a person. Of course, these are false gods. God said, "Thou shalt have no other gods before Me." (Ex. 20:3) He is jealous and we should beware of His wrath.

Religious extremists are in every nation and culture. Some aren't religious; they're mean and evil. Children have killed others and themselves. Violent video games are sometimes blamed. Some should refrain from brutal games and study their Bible. We should set better examples for children; God requires it.

This country was founded on Godly principals. Everyone has freedom of religion, if they don't violate rights of others. A religion that promotes murder and suicide is misguided. They use control and brainwashing. Children and adults are taught to murder and commit suicide. God forgives anything, except resisting His forgiveness. If we reject Him, we have committed the unpardonable sin. Whosoever will—can follow Jesus Christ and be saved!

Most false prophets are careful about not breaking laws, but some aren't. Crimes are committed in religions because, it's difficult and in most cases impossible to prosecute. Yet preachers can be charged with a hate crime for preaching the truth. Our criminal justice system needs revising. It was originally designed by following God's Word. If people don't turn back to God, we may cease to be a nation.

Karen was exposed to false teaching, control, and brainwashing. It was detrimental to her spiritual, and physical health. If someone asked me, "Do you believe false prophets killed Karen?" My reply would be, "Indirectly." That would be an affirmative. Unfortunately, I can't prosecute.

Many factors led to Karen's death. Two were religion and false prophets. She had the freedom to walk away. She could have drawn closer to God and His Word. Karen made the mistakes most people make, including me. She relied too much on teachers and preachers. The Holy Ghost is the best teacher. He teaches everything we need.

We pretty much determine how long we live by the way we live. Jesus recommends life more abundantly. Accept Him by faith as Lord and Savior. Eat and drink properly, rest, exercise, work smarter, and ask Him for whatever you need. Be careful and avoid accidents. Beware of false prophets. Above all be happy, and don't worry. Talk to your spouse and spend quality time with them. You may find the elusive dream—called happiness.

Five types of false prophets are mentioned in this story. The first type is extremists. Certain factions in any nation or society have perverted decency and common sense. Some are religious and some secular. They are evil and wouldn't receive this label. They think they're holy and Godly. Secular ones just believe they're good. Some are taught to hate, kill others and themselves. Religious ones think others are evil, if their beliefs differ. In their reasoning, murder and suicide are rewarded with eternal life in heaven. God doesn't reward murder; He can forgive it. They could change and be led by God's Holy Spirit into heaven.

The second type is in the non-denominational religions. There are churches in those religions that I highly respect; they don't get into emotionalism. Teaching others to fall and seeking signs and wonders is wrong. This opens the door to demonic activity.

We don't know when someone crosses the line and becomes a false prophet. Make sure you aren't misled. Remember, a disciple or student will be like his teacher. Jesus declared that in Luke 6:40.

All churches make mistakes; make sure they aren't too dreadful. If they won't change, we have other options, one being—change churches. Let God direct your paths. Don't lean to your ideas; acknowledge Him in all your ways.

The third type is in some denominational churches. They take away from the words in the Bible, and at times add to them. They teach rules, traditions, and commandments of men as if they were doctrines of God. If we aren't careful, we'll resemble the scribes and Pharisees. They were religious and thought they were holy. Jesus explained to them; they were of their father the devil. "...except your righteousness shall exceed the righteousness of the scribes and Pharisees ye shall in no case enter into the kingdom of heaven." (Mt. 5:20)

The fourth type is lay people of the church or those who don't attend church. People who don't preach or teach, can instruct in a wrong way. If we are dogmatic about God or His Word, we may be leading ourself and others into trouble.

Begin reading the Gospel of John, also First, Second and Third John. Study Romans and Corinthians. Read Proverbs, and Psalms. Study the New Testament. Read the Old, but the New is the better covenant!

The fifth type is called cults. Most lead people away from the teachings of Jesus Christ. They have become anti Christ. Jesus Christ is the one and only way to eternal life. Some sell everything they own and give it to an organization—that intends to disown them unless they totally submit. Do you think they give back the property? Please beware of religions that kill, steal and destroy. Good religions give; they don't take.

How do false prophets kill? I'll list the methods I'm aware of. False prophets can discourage us by saying all churches are wrong. That isn't true. Churches make mistakes because they're operated by imperfect people. Don't be offended by this and gain all the good you can. If we don't attend church, we could backslide, never repent and spend eternity in hell. Hebrews chapter ten explains this.

The first or natural death can be caused by false prophets. They teach adding things to the Bible. By doing this, plagues such as a heart attack etc. can kill. False prophets cause confusion, stress and worry. People can be overcome with despair and commit suicide. Jim Jones persuaded his followers to drink poison and they died. Some teach murder and suicide. Obviously, this causes death. Confusion and stress can cause fatal accidents. We need peace, so we can enter God's rest. Find this in Hebrews chapter four. We won't have to work hard, or worry ourselves to death.

Denominational false prophets take away from the words of the Bible. Revelation 22:19 clearly explains this. "And if any man shall take away from the words of the book of this prophecy, God shall take away his part out of the book of life, and out of the holy city, and from the things which are written in this book." If our Father in heaven takes our part from the things written in the Bible, guess what? Salvation is written there. Those who teach others to misinterpret scriptures can cause them to have their names—blotted or taken out of the book of life. It's the worst way a false prophet can kill you and it is avoidable!

We Do Not Have To Experience The Second Death

Hell is considered by the Bible, the second death. The second death is much worse than the natural one. Everyone must experience death because we have sinned. However, we don't have to experience the second death. Don't let false prophets kill you in this manner.

Jesus is the way, the truth, and the life. Wide and broad is the way that leads to hell. Most people will go that way. The way is narrow that leads to heaven. It will only be found by few. If millions of people make it to heaven, it will be a few compared to the billions that have lived on earth. Jesus taught; most people won't go to heaven. They are deceived by the wide and broad ways. (paraphrasing Mt. 7:13–14)

Why do you think most people won't make it to heaven? Jesus made it plain in the next verse. Mt. 7:15 says, "Beware of false prophets, which come to you in sheep's clothing, but inwardly they are ravening wolves." Notice the next verse. "Ye shall know them by their fruits." They seem like Christians, but they are not. We know them by their actions. There are two directions that lead to eternity. Take the narrow way, not the broad. One way leads to heaven. Many ways lead to hell; it's our choice and His offer still stands.

With thousands of religions in the world, and variations within each one, the wrong ways are incredibly wide and broad. Can you perceive why the way is narrow that leads to eternal life? Can you see why the ways that lead to destruction are wide and broad?

Jesus made it plain; false teachers, false prophets, and people who teach wrong traditions of men won't go to heaven. I will have a Bible study with anyone. I'll be alone, but you can bring friends, teachers or a preacher. If you prove me wrong on anything, or a number of points, I will change my writings and publicly apologize. I would gladly mention your name, or

176

the names of your group if you desire. I want to know if I'm wrong, so I can repent and get on the right track.

My apology would appear in The Taylorsville Times. If you reside in another city, you could reprint my letter in your local newspaper. The Taylorsville Times is on the internet. I won't respond with a letter to the editor. That is not a proper way to resolve spiritual differences.

I recommend the baptism of the Holy Ghost. If you want to walk in the Spirit, ask God to help. "God is a Spirit and they that worship him must worship him in spirit and in truth." (John 4:24) Praying in the Spirit is biblical. Doubt, fear, and unbelief will cause us to come up short every time. Trust, have faith and believe. Don't be ashamed of the Holy Ghost; receive Him and anything that He recommends. Be careful of people, churches and traditions you follow. Embrace good traditions and avoid the bad ones like a plague.

We should be of one mind and one accord. There is no better way— than to have the same spirit, His Spirit. There should be unity in the body of Christ. We are members of His body and must love one another.

A woman often made the statement—you are saved if you live it. A man often makes this statement. "It doesn't matter who is right; what matters is—what is right."

How do you think it's possible to acknowledge Jesus Christ as the head of the church? (Follow His Word) Some think pastors, deacons or a few wealthy families should be the head of the church. The Bible says, Jesus is. Since we can't see Him, we must listen to Him through His Word. He is here in Spirit! Christians have the Holy Spirit inside them. He speaks through our good thoughts—if we know how to listen.

Misguided elders or deacons show partiality, control people and make threats. This causes people to quit church. Of course they deny any allegation of running off others. Leaders like that desire to increase their support. They make sure a vote by the church, will go their way. Christians who are sweet and kind will usually leave quietly without telling anyone how they were treated. It's no surprise most churches have problems. Good people are run off for no good reason. God wants us to reconcile our differences, love and forgive one another. Churches should grow—not decrease!

Unfortunately, we have pastors who use the same mean tricks on people they claim to love. When someone sins against us, the Bible tells us what to do. We are to confront the person in private. If the problem can't be resolved, we should try again with one or two witnesses. We should be gentle during the process. Hopefully the problem won't have to be brought before the church. The congregation is the final arbitrator in such matters. They should decide according to what God's Word says. I am paraphrasing Jesus Christ in (Mt. 18:15–17)

THERE IS ONLY ONE WHO IS ALWAYS RIGHT,

JESUS CHRIST!